Adolescence: A Very Short Introduction

VERY SHORT INTRODUCTIONS are for anyone wanting a stimulating and accessible way into a new subject. They are written by experts, and have been translated into more than 40 different languages.

The series began in 1995, and now covers a wide variety of topics in every discipline. The VSI library now contains over 450 volumes—a Very Short Introduction to everything from Psychology and Philosophy of Science to American History and Relativity—and continues to grow in every subject area.

Very Short Introductions available now:

ACCOUNTING Christopher Nobes
ADOLESCENCE Peter K. Smith
ADVERTISING Winston Fletcher
AFRICAN AMERICAN RELIGION
   Eddie S. Glaude Jr
AFRICAN HISTORY John Parker and
   Richard Rathbone
AFRICAN RELIGIONS Jacob K. Olupona
AGNOSTICISM Robin Le Poidevin
AGRICULTURE Paul Brassley and
   Richard Soffe
ALEXANDER THE GREAT
   Hugh Bowden
ALGEBRA Peter M. Higgins
AMERICAN HISTORY Paul S. Boyer
AMERICAN IMMIGRATION
   David A. Gerber
AMERICAN LEGAL HISTORY
   G. Edward White
AMERICAN POLITICAL HISTORY
   Donald Critchlow
AMERICAN POLITICAL PARTIES
   AND ELECTIONS L. Sandy Maisel
AMERICAN POLITICS Richard M. Valelly
THE AMERICAN PRESIDENCY
   Charles O. Jones
THE AMERICAN REVOLUTION
   Robert J. Allison
AMERICAN SLAVERY
   Heather Andrea Williams
THE AMERICAN WEST Stephen Aron
AMERICAN WOMEN'S HISTORY
   Susan Ware
ANAESTHESIA Aidan O'Donnell
ANARCHISM Colin Ward

ANCIENT ASSYRIA Karen Radner
ANCIENT EGYPT Ian Shaw
ANCIENT EGYPTIAN ART AND
   ARCHITECTURE Christina Riggs
ANCIENT GREECE Paul Cartledge
THE ANCIENT NEAR EAST
   Amanda H. Podany
ANCIENT PHILOSOPHY Julia Annas
ANCIENT WARFARE Harry Sidebottom
ANGELS David Albert Jones
ANGLICANISM Mark Chapman
THE ANGLO-SAXON AGE John Blair
THE ANIMAL KINGDOM
   Peter Holland
ANIMAL RIGHTS David DeGrazia
THE ANTARCTIC Klaus Dodds
ANTISEMITISM Steven Beller
ANXIETY Daniel Freeman and
   Jason Freeman
THE APOCRYPHAL GOSPELS
   Paul Foster
ARCHAEOLOGY Paul Bahn
ARCHITECTURE Andrew Ballantyne
ARISTOCRACY William Doyle
ARISTOTLE Jonathan Barnes
ART HISTORY Dana Arnold
ART THEORY Cynthia Freeland
ASTROBIOLOGY David C. Catling
ASTROPHYSICS James Binney
ATHEISM Julian Baggini
AUGUSTINE Henry Chadwick
AUSTRALIA Kenneth Morgan
AUTISM Uta Frith
THE AVANT GARDE David Cottington
THE AZTECS David Carrasco

For more information visit our website

www.oup.com/vsi/

Peter K. Smith

ADOLESCENCE

A Very Short Introduction

OXFORD
UNIVERSITY PRESS

OXFORD
UNIVERSITY PRESS

Great Clarendon Street, Oxford, OX2 6DP,
United Kingdom

Oxford University Press is a department of the University of Oxford.
It furthers the University's objective of excellence in research, scholarship,
and education by publishing worldwide. Oxford is a registered trade mark of
Oxford University Press in the UK and in certain other countries

© Peter K. Smith 2016

The moral rights of the author have been asserted

First edition published in 2016

Impression: 1

Published in the United States of America by Oxford University Press
198 Madison Avenue, New York, NY 10016, United States of America

British Library Cataloguing in Publication Data
Data available

Library of Congress Control Number: 2015958364

ISBN 978-0-19-966556-3

Printed in Great Britain by
Ashford Colour Press Ltd, Gosport, Hampshire

Contents

List of illustrations

List of tables

Chapter 1
Adolescence as a life stage

Adolescence is a period of transition between life as a child, and life as an adult. Biologically, entrance into adolescence can be marked by the onset of puberty, and most dictionaries define it as the period following the onset of puberty during which a young person develops from a child into an adult. After puberty, a person is sexually mature and could potentially become a mother or father of a child. Socially, adolescence can be marked by an increasing independence from parents, an increasing importance of the peer group, and often aspects such as mood swings, conflicts with parents, and risky or reckless behaviours—what has been called the 'storm and stress' of the adolescent period. The end of adolescence can be less clear than the onset, but as the young person prepares to complete his or her education, to form sexual partnerships, to seek some vocation or employment, and often to leave home, the achievement of these can be taken as markers of adult life being reached.

In modern Western societies, adolescence has been basically thought of as covering the teenage years. However the earlier advent of puberty means that many researchers take it as being from around 10-18 years, and the World Health Organization defines it as from ages 10 to 19. Also, a period of emerging adulthood has been proposed before full adulthood is reached (Chapter 8).

Adolescence has some universal features, notably puberty and its associated changes, but the nature and even the timing of adolescence shows important cultural and historical variations. It has been studied from many disciplinary perspectives. Those working from the perspective of evolutionary theory generally emphasize the universal aspects of adolescence. Such arguments may be complemented by recent perspectives from developmental neuroscience. On the other hand, historians, anthropologists, and sociologists tend to emphasize the more variable features of adolescence and may question many universal aspects. Some even see adolescence as a social construction. Psychologists (and I come from this discipline primarily) may span a range of such views, from evolutionary developmental psychology through to cultural psychology. This chapter starts with an overview of these different approaches.

The evolution of human adolescence

Evolutionary theory developed from the work of Charles Darwin in the latter half of the 19th century, but has been elaborated in many ways over the next hundred years. A central perspective has been how behaviour is selected for the ultimate aim of reproductive success—the passing on of genetic material to the next generation. Behaviours that enhance reproductive success are seen as adaptive for the individual. While this does imply competition between individuals, it can also bring about cooperation through mechanisms such as kin selection (helping others who are genetically related) and reciprocal altruism (helping others who help you in return).

The reference point for this adaptativeness is taken as the environment that humans evolved in over many thousands of years. This is sometimes called the *environment of evolutionary adaptedness*. It is generally taken as being the kind of hunter-gatherer existence that characterized most of human evolution. Settled agricultural and then urban life, which are quite different, are seen as relatively recent cultural changes which have not had very much influence on our genetic heritage. As a consequence, some of our genetic adaptations may not be so well adapted to contemporary living. For example, hunter-gatherers make the most of sweet foods such as honey when they find them; but a genetic predisposition to love sweet foods can lead to obesity in modern environments where they are readily available.

A number of theorists, such as Glenn Weisfeld and Melvin Konner in the first decade of this century, have written about adolescence from the perspective of evolutionary theory. Two aspects particularly important for adolescence are *life history theory* and *sexual selection theory*.

Life history theory examines why there are certain stages through the life cycle and why they last for certain periods. For example, compared to other primates (monkeys and apes), human infants are born relatively helpless and need a long period of protected infancy, provided by parents and kin. Also, compared to other primates, there is a long period between this protected infancy period and the onset of reproductive maturity at puberty. This period of middle childhood lasts some eight to ten years. Given the greatly increased brain size in humans, and the importance of culture (language, tool use, social customs), this extended childhood period is seen as necessary for cultural learning before the serious business of seeking mates and having offspring.

Adolescence is a period characterized by a second growth spurt in the life cycle (the first being in the prenatal period), and the onset of puberty (Chapter 2). Whereas childhood can be seen as a period of cultural learning from parents and elders, adolescence can be seen as a period of finding one's place in a similar age peer group and preparing for having offspring. One aspect of human puberty is adolescent sterility, namely that female fertility is relatively low in the years immediately following puberty. This can be argued to

3

be adaptive in terms of becoming more mature before the considerable burden of raising offspring is incurred.

An evolutionary perspective predicts that with puberty and the arrival of the potential for reproduction, direct strategies for optimizing reproductive success will come to the fore. Such strategies could be cooperative or competitive. Cooperative strategies might involve alliances within the peer group, consistent with increased anxiety about friendships and conformity to peer pressure. Competitive strategies might involve more concern about status with same-sex and opposite-sex peers, consistent with increases in behaviours such as bullying and delinquency.

Sexual selection theory delineates how different strategies would be predicted to be advantageous for the two sexes. This is because competition for mates and reproductive success is greater in males than females. This is something generally true of mammals, where the variation in number of offspring is much greater in males than females. This is true in humans too. For example, the Mongol leader Genghis Khan has been calculated (through DNA evidence) to be an ancestor of some 8 per cent of men currently living in the regions of Asia that was the former Mongol empire. This is thought to be because one man could have many wives, and other opportunities for mating as well through conquest.

Puberty in humans is characterized by *sexual bimaturism*, meaning that the timing differs between the sexes. It normally starts some two years earlier in girls. Evolutionary theorists argue that it is more advantageous for males to delay puberty until their growth spurt has made them bigger and stronger and better able to compete with others. The sexes also differ somewhat in the physical and psychological consequences of puberty, in ways which would have been adaptive, at least for much of human evolution. Increased strength and size, and increased competitiveness, would have been important for boys especially, for hunting and fighting skills. Increased reckless behaviour could be seen as display to demonstrate status and prowess, and attract the opposite sex. Competitiveness in girls would not take such physical forms (as physical strength was less important for them), but instead would take more relational forms, such as damaging others' friendships and reputation. Also, increased manual dexterity in girls, and increased interest in infants, would have been important for gathering skills and future caregiving.

Aspects of behaviour such as more frequent or serious conflicts with parents (Chapter 4) and increased risk-taking behaviours (Chapter 6) can be seen from an evolutionary perspective as often adaptive for the individual adolescent, even if annoying or deleterious for the wider society. A general point here is that what are often called problem behaviours in adolescence may be seen as problems by others but may often be advantageous, at least in the short term or in some circumstances, for the adolescents involved.

Critics of the evolutionary approach suggest that the adaptive explanations advanced are often glib, untested, and justify the status quo of existing Western society (e.g. greater competitiveness in males). They also suggest that human behaviour (including at adolescence) is much more flexible than the evolutionary perspective allows for. While these critiques have some force, in fact many predictions from evolutionary theory are testable, and the approach is quite compatible with there being degrees of cultural variation. As an example, the onset of puberty varies considerably between individuals, and this has received attention from life history theorists. Here, the argument is about which strategies—early or late onset of puberty—are most adaptive in certain types of environmental situations (resource availability, dependability of partners and kin). These arguments (Chapter 2) demonstrate that an evolutionary perspective is not only compatible with the idea of a genetic blueprint being strongly influenced by environmental effects, but can make predictions about what such effects might be. Nevertheless there is seen to be a blueprint—the evolutionary view is incompatible with a 'blank slate' view of human nature.

Anthropological and sociological perspectives

Anthropologists have, over the last century especially, documented life in pre-industrial societies. The organized study of such societies started in the early 20th century. A leading exponent, Franz Boas, explicitly rejected ideas of biological determinism, which had had some prominence with the advent of Darwin's ideas. In fact, Boas could be described as a cultural determinist.

The first major study of adolescence in a non-Western culture was carried out by Margaret Mead, in Samoa, in the 1920s. Mead was a student of Boas, and Boas had set her the task of answering the questions: 'Are the disturbances which vex our adolescents due to the nature of adolescence itself or to the civilization? Under different conditions does adolescence present a different pattern?' Mead knew that Boas expected the answers 'the civilization' and 'yes' to these questions, and this is what she duly provided in a famous book, *Coming of Age in Samoa*, published in 1928. It had a huge impact at the time and for some decades to come.

This book is still worth reading today and, on the positive side, it is probably the first serious and well documented attempt to understand the experiences of children and adolescents growing up in a non-Western society. Indeed, Mead, who also had a Master's degree in child psychology, has been recognized as a pioneer in this respect. The picture she painted of adolescence was very different indeed from that common in North American or indeed Western society generally, at that time (and also now). Rather than a troubled period, with greater conflict with parents, Mead stated that in Samoa, adolescence was 'the age of maximum ease', with 'an absence of psychological maladjustment'. Samoan society was 'replete with easy solutions for all conflicts'. For example, since Samoans had an open and extended family-rearing system, an adolescent who might be in disagreement with parents could easily go and stay with another relative. In addition, she wrote that Samoan society 'never exerts sufficient repression to call forth a significant rebellion from the individual'. There was no guilt about sexual behaviour and experimentation before marriage, and there was little for adolescents to rebel against; they had 'the sunniest and easiest attitudes towards sex', and promiscuity and free love were the norm in the adolescent period.

This is about as different from a storm and stress model of adolescence as one could imagine. Mead's work, and that of other anthropologists who worked with Boas such as Ruth Benedict, supported a view that the experience of adolescence was entirely a matter of social structure and cultural pressures. The biological impact of puberty was of little consequence. As Boas put it: 'much of what we ascribe to human nature is no more than a reaction to the restraints put upon us by our civilization'.

Criticisms of Mead's work in Samoa came to a head some sixty years later, after Mead had died (in 1978). An Australian anthropologist, Derek Freeman, argued that her methodology had been poor. For example she did not properly learn the native language, and it is not clear how much trust or rapport she had with the adolescents whom she interviewed about very sensitive matters such as sexual experience. Indeed, Freeman managed to track down, many years later, an elderly Samoan lady, Fa'apua'a Fa'amu, who had apparently been one of Mead's two principal female adolescent informants. Fa'amu testified that much of what she had related to Mead, for example about early sexual experiences, had been made up as a kind of joke. Freeman also argued that other studies of Samoa give a different overall picture from Mead's. Not all researchers agree with all Freeman's criticisms, but they have certainly cast major doubt on Mead's conclusions about how adolescence in Samoa was totally different from Western expectations.

In the fifty years following Mead's work, many accounts had been written of life in pre-industrial societies across the globe. Records from 186 such societies were gathered in the Standard Cross-Cultural Sample in 1980. These show many differences regarding adolescence in different cultures, but also some common features, as a quantitative analysis by Schlegel and Barry in 1991 demonstrated. Of course, these societies have been changing rapidly through the influences of colonization and later globalization, but they do provide accounts of what life was like before such influences produced the radical changes obvious in the 21st century.

From such records and analyses, it seems that only about one-third of societies had a particular linguistic marker corresponding to *adolescent*. However the period was generally marked in clear behavioural ways. The majority of societies, nearly three-quarters, had some sort of public initiation ceremony, typically different for boys and girls. In 87 per cent of the societies studied, girls were initiated singly, at the onset of menarche. However in more than half of the societies, boys were initiated in groups, or age-cohorts. While often triggered by puberty, this was not always the case.

For example, among the Mardujara Aboriginal people of Australia, studied during the 1960s, male initiation was a complex procedure enacted by elders of the tribe, often on several boys at the same time (who were around puberty but sometimes varying in age by two or three years). The rituals included nose piercing, circumcision, a journey to other camps, and a period of seclusion. Each boy was initiated into various sacred aspects of tribal practices, and had to carve several sacred boards in wood. He was then considered ready to get married to a girl previously promised to him.

Initiation of girls in traditional societies was often less public, but could also include very painful practices such as female circumcision (now called female genital mutilation, FGM, or cutting, FGM/C). A classic ethnographic study by Otto Raum in 1940, on the Chaga people of what is now Tanzania, described this practice in some detail. The older generation justified such practices in terms of religious tradition, and purifying the girl to make her ready for marriage. By and large, different cultural practices are accepted as valid in a particular culture, but FGM is now condemned by the World Health Organization, and criminalized in all member states of the European Union. This is an outstanding example of how universal ideas of human rights may come into conflict with certain cultural traditions.

Generally, initiation rituals were important in signalling the transition from child to adult, and breaking the close link children had previously had with the mother. The young person might learn important knowledge or practise skills needed for adult life. The rituals also reinforced the authority of the tribal elders who performed the ceremonies. It is also thought that the group nature of many male initiation rites was important in forging male solidarity among young men who would need to cooperate in hunting and fighting activities in their adult life.

In these traditional societies, following puberty there was often a period of from two to four years for boys, but up to about two years for girls, before the end of adolescence, as typically marked by marriage and then child-rearing. Girls were often married at a younger age than boys. Schlegel and Barry called this period between sexual maturity and full social maturity *social adolescence*. They summarized that this period 'appears to be universal for boys; for girls, in the majority of societies, at least a short period of adolescence intervenes between puberty and the full assumption of adult roles, usually at marriage'. A period of apprenticeship, in which specialized skills were learnt from older craftsmen, might be typical of this period (Figure 1).

While marriage was always heterosexual, there was considerable variation in sexual practices in traditional societies. Many

1. An adolescent apprentice cabinet maker in Ngozi, Burundi, learns from an adult mentor.

permitted or sometimes encouraged some degree of homosexual behaviour, especially during the adolescent period. However this was described as usually being of a casual and transient nature.

Sociologists have provided an analysis of modern societies, including the nature of adolescence. Theorists such as Glen Elder have pointed out how the historical time and place can have a profound influence on development, for example in the USA looking at the impact of historical events such as the Great Depression in the 1930s and World War II in the 1940s. A major contrast between modern societies and traditional societies has been the advent of universal schooling, through the 20th century. Many young people now spend the whole of their teenage years, and often beyond, in full-time education. Adult work roles, marriage, and child-rearing are generally delayed until such education is completed, and school-leaving or college graduation can be seen as a modern rite of passage into adulthood. Thus the period of social adolescence is greatly extended. In addition, adolescents typically find themselves in much larger same-age peer groups than would be typical in traditional societies. Recreational possibilities have also changed dramatically, through organized sports, television, music groups, and more recently the internet (Chapter 5). Many of these changes are likely to decrease the traditional authority of the older generation and increase the influence of the peer group (Chapter 4).

Historical perspectives

Historians of childhood have focused on developments in European societies, which are well documented from classical times, but especially through the medieval period and into the early modern period. The term *adolescence* comes from Latin, meaning 'growing or coming to maturity', and in Middle French (15th century) it meant 'a youth'. The term, and the concept, were clearly present in earlier historical periods.

In contrast, the French historian Philippe Ariès argued in his book *Centuries of Childhood* (English translation in 1962) that adolescence came into being as a concept in the 18th century, and that in the Middle Ages children mixed in with adults once they were out of the infancy period. However, his view was largely based on limited evidence, such as analyses of paintings of upper class families, and his views have been extensively criticized by many historians. They were described as 'simplistic and inaccurate' by Barbara Hanawalt thirty years later, on the basis of much more direct evidence of the lives of children and young people in historical times.

However, Hanawalt argued that the nature or definition of adolescence had changed a lot over the centuries. In particular, the ages of entrance into and exit from the adolescent period could vary greatly. During the medieval period girls could marry as young as 12 and boys at 14, and this sometimes happened, although more usually it was considerably delayed. One factor delaying marriage, especially for males, was the common practice of serving as an apprentice for a trade, or a servant for a richer family. Only once this was completed, sometimes not until well into one's 20s, would marriage normally happen. A common feature throughout the medieval period in Europe is described by Hanawalt as the manipulation or control by adults of the nature and duration of this adolescent period. This in itself could be a source of conflict. In early modern times, Shakespeare has an old shepherd say in *The Winter's Tale*, written in 1611, 'I would there were no age between ten and three-and-twenty, or that youth would sleep out the rest; for there is nothing in the between but getting wenches with child, wronging the ancientry, stealing, fighting'.

The 19th and 20th centuries saw great changes in the Western economies, with the industrial revolution, and then subsequent improvements in health care and education. These have impacted on adolescence in various ways, some mentioned earlier, but also including the age of onset of puberty (Chapter 2), adolescent mental health (Chapter 7), and sexual attitudes and behaviour (Chapter 8).

Psychological perspectives

One important origin of psychological thinking about adolescence is in the work of G. Stanley Hall at the start of the 20th century. Hall was awarded the first doctorate in psychology in the United States, and founded the *American Journal of Psychology*. In 1904 he published a two-volume collection entitled *Adolescence*. This was influenced by Darwin's ideas, and also the now discredited theory that ontogeny (individual development) recapitulated phylogeny (evolution).

In these books he introduced the phrase *storm and stress* to characterize adolescence. Three aspects of this were conflict with parents, mood disruption, and risky behaviour—themes still resonant a century later.

2. Sigmund Freud, G. Stanley Hall, and Carl Jung (front row) at Clark University, 1909.

Another influence during the first half of the 20th century was psychoanalysis. Interestingly, Hall invited both Sigmund Freud and Carl Jung to give lectures at Clark University, where he worked, in 1909—Freud's only visit to the USA (Figure 2). Freud's view of human psychosexual development was that following the repression of unacceptable sexual impulses early in childhood, there was a latency period from about 5 years of age to puberty. However, at puberty there was a renewed upsurge of sexual instincts that reawakened conflicts that had not been resolved earlier. Thus Freud's view and that of later psychoanalysts was congruent with a storm and stress view of adolescence. They came at this from different premises than Hall. However, in both traditions, hormonal changes were commonly implicated as an immediate causal mechanism in the changes.

Such psychoanalytic theories received much criticism from psychologists later in the 20th century. They generally rejected recapitulation theory and also the idea of sexual instincts. However, a revision of the psychoanalytic approach made by Erik Erikson attracted more support, being based on giving a much larger role to cultural influences in personality formation. Erikson particularly emphasized the identity crisis in adolescence (Chapter 4). The idea of adolescence as a turbulent, rebellious period continued to be widely held into the 1960s and 1970s. However in the later 1970s and 1980s more researchers stressed the view that the conflicts in adolescence were by no means universal, and were often minor and about mundane matters.

Over the last two decades, some psychologists have re-asserted earlier ideas around adolescence as a time of turmoil, albeit in more measured ways. Jeffrey Arnett concluded that storm and stress is 'a real part of life for many adolescents and their parents'. However he also remarked on strong cultural variations in the three aspects of this that Hall had proposed. He drew a comparison between narrow and broad socialization patterns. Narrow socialization is characterized by firm expectations of, and restrictions on, adolescent behaviour, typical of pre-industrial societies. Family, peers, and community act to reduce reckless behaviour, though at the expense of greater conformity and less independence and creativity. Conversely, broad socialization is characterized by few personal restrictions, and more expectations of self-expression and autonomy, typical of modern Western societies. There is less conformity and more creativity, but greater reckless behaviour.

Developmental neuroscience

The last decade especially has seen a rapid growth in developmental neuroscience, facilitated by specialist techniques such as neuroimaging. These enable us to assess neural activity in different areas of the brain, when someone is engaged with particular thoughts or experiences. It has become clear that there are significant brain changes going on, around puberty (Chapter 2). This is especially marked in the frontal cortex.

Sarah-Jayne Blakemore argued in 2014 that this brain remodelling especially involves a set of regions, called the social brain, that affect emotional regulation, response inhibition, and planning. Neuroimaging studies have shown that these areas are particularly activated during social cognitive tasks related to perspective-taking and impulse control, processing emotional states of others, concern for self vs. ideas of trust and sharing, peer influence, peer evaluation, and fear of rejection (Chapter 4). It is argued that the brain areas mediating such emotions change more rapidly than those mediating cognitive regulation. Such differential changes have been used to explain greater self-focus in adolescence, greater reward-seeking, and increased risk-taking (Chapter 5). This area of neuroscience research on the adolescent brain is developing rapidly and leading to important insights. The findings integrate well with the more traditional views on social and cognitive changes, but also open up new possibilities for understanding and intervention.

Chapter 2
Puberty—body and brain changes

As children become teenagers, their bodies change dramatically. An obvious change is the *growth spurt*. After a period of rather steady growth through middle childhood at around 5-6 cm in height per year, the rate of growth increases early on in puberty. It reaches about 9 cm per year in girls and 10 cm per year in boys before falling off sharply a few years later. This sudden acceleration in the rate of gaining height, and also of putting on weight, typically happens faster in the legs than the torso, and the young person often feels lanky and awkward. In addition, breast development starts for girls. Also there are voice changes, notably deepening for boys; and skin changes, such as acne.

Besides these changes that are obvious to everyone, the genitalia are enlarging and the young person is becoming reproductively mature. These processes start in the early adolescent period (around 11-14 years) and are largely complete by middle adolescence (around 14-16 years). Girls go through puberty some eighteen months before boys do. However there are large individual variations. Some main signs of pubertal development in boys and girls, with approximate average ages at which they are reached, are shown in Table 1.

Table 1. Some main signs of pubertal development in boys and girls, with approximate average ages at which they are reached

Age range	Girls	Boys
9–10	Budding of breasts	
10–11	Growth spurt begins Pubic hair appears	
11–12	Growth of genitalia	First growth of testes, and later penis
12–13	Breasts fill out Menarche	Growth spurt begins
13–14	Growth spurt tails off	Facial hair Spermache
14–15	Earliest normal pregnancies	Voice deepening
15–16	Voice deepening	Growth spurt tails off
16+	Puberty largely completed, although some further physical growth may continue into early adulthood.	

Why does puberty happen?

Puberty involves a set of somewhat synchronized changes, occurring over a few years. This is a common, species-specific pattern. In evolutionary terms, young people become reproductively mature when their bodies and minds have grown sufficiently that they are able not only to have children themselves, but to look after them with some success. The growth spurt, together with neural and cognitive changes, helps to prepare them for this.

The bodily changes in puberty are produced by increased levels of growth hormones and sex hormones circulating via the blood. These hormones do circulate earlier in life; younger children grow and they do have (immature) genitalia. But at adolescence these hormones circulate at much higher levels. They are produced by the pituitary gland, directly, in the case of growth hormones, and indirectly (via the adrenal cortex and the gonads— testes and ovaries), in the case of sex hormones. The pituitary gland is in turn controlled by the hypothalamus, a small but very important structure at the base of the forebrain.

Regarding puberty, the hypothalamus acts rather like a thermostat controlling room temperature; at the onset of puberty the setting changes, causing the pituitary gland to work harder, leading to the production of more growth and sex hormones until a new, stable (but higher) level is reached. The growth hormones produce the physical changes such as the growth spurt; the sex hormones (notably androgen, testosterone, oestrogen, and progesterone) produce changes in the genitalia and in secondary sexual characteristics (not directly concerned with reproduction) such as enlargement of the breasts in females and growth of body hair.

The measurement of puberty

Much work on typical patterns of physical development in adolescence was carried out at the Institute of Child Health in London in the 1960s and 1970s. Led by James Tanner, one outcome was the development of Tanner diagrams; some similar examples are shown in Figure 3. A full version has a graded set of figures showing changes in the genitalia, breast development, and pubic hair. An individual young person can then be matched on this scale, which gives what are known as 'Tanner stages'. More direct measurements can also be made, for example of testicular volume in boys.

The Tanner diagrams give a scaled measure of how far puberty has progressed. There are two other common methods which give an age of pubertal onset. For girls, their first period is a very clear indicator of reproductive maturity, even though some period of adolescent infertility does mean that pregnancies very soon after

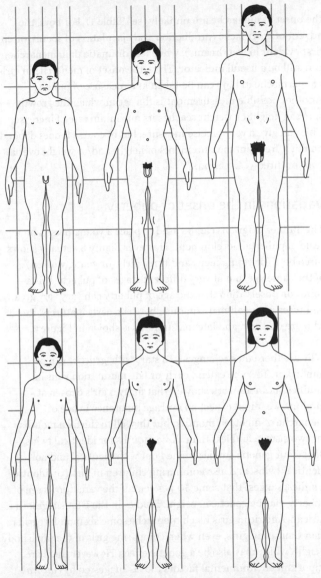

3. Tanner diagrams showing individual variations in pubertal development for (a) three boys all aged 14¾ years; and (b) three girls all aged 12¾ years.

the onset of menarche are unlikely (see Table 1). For boys, the advent of spermache (production and ejaculation of sperm, often first evident in wet dreams), while less dramatic than menarche, can still be a useful indicator. Thus, the onset of menarche in girls or spermache in boys can be taken as a measure of puberty. Another possible measurement is the age at which the growth spurt in height or weight reaches its maximum rate of increase. This can give a very precise measure, but of course it does depend on fairly frequent measurements of height and/or weight over a two- or three-year period.

Variations in the onset of puberty

The Tanner diagrams can be used to place a young person on a scale of pubertal development. However Figure 3 actually shows three boys (or young men) and three girls (or young women) of the same age, but at very different stages of puberty. It is a common observation that the age of puberty can vary very greatly, and researchers often distinguish between early maturers, those who are on-time, and late maturers, as is shown in Figure 3.

Why are there these changes? To start with, *genetics* can be important. To some extent, early or late maturation runs in families. Tanner's work showed that for two girls chosen at random, we might expect an average difference in age of menarche of nineteen months; but this fell to thirteen months for two sisters, and less than three months for identical twins. Behaviour genetic studies carried out with identical and non-identical twins, and also comparing children in birth or adoptive families, suggest that some 50 per cent of the variation in age of puberty may be genetic in origin. Studies in the USA suggest that African-American girls reach menarche some six months earlier than Caucasian girls, even when comparing girls of the same body weight, which may also be a genetic effect. However there are important environmental factors too, as suggested by *cultural* and *social class differences*. In many African countries, puberty is delayed, probably because of the effects of poorer nutrition. Poorer nutrition is also the likely explanation for delayed puberty associated with lower socioeconomic status. In fact there is plentiful evidence that *nutrition* and *physical activity* can affect the onset of puberty. Most of this evidence is recent, but one historical study went back to the 18th century. This analysed records of voice changes in choirboys at the cathedral in Leipzig where Bach was musical director. The boys' change of voice then occurred rather late compared to boys nowadays, at around 17 years (see the secular trend, in the next section). Voice change was delayed even more during a famine which occurred mid-century. In explaining the effects of malnutrition, it has been suggested that it is necessary to reach a certain level of body weight growth, and especially a threshold value of relative fatness, to go into puberty. This seems to be even more true for girls entering menarche, which of course makes biological sense. It would also explain why some female athletes who are training very rigorously may experience periods of amenorrhea (cessation of periods) if they go below this relative fatness threshold.

A recent concern has been the possible impact of *endocrine disrupting compounds* or EDCs. These are compounds that interfere with endocrine action and hormone production. They may be synthetic (e.g. insecticides) or natural (e.g. lead or other heavy metal compounds). The presence of EDCs in the diet or in the environment has raised concerns about decreased sperm counts in recent years. They may also affect the onset and process of puberty, although the nature of this (acceleration, delay, or disruption) does vary between studies.

Some theorists viewing puberty in an evolutionary and life-history perspective have looked at the 'costs' and 'benefits' of early or late puberty, and posit the importance of *early family experiences.* The psychosocial acceleration theory suggests that some kinds of psychosocial stress, and especially low parental investment and/or stressful early family circumstances such as parental conflict and divorce, bring forward the onset of puberty. This theory proposes that in a stable, relatively predictable and secure environment, it is best to only enter puberty once fully ready and in a position to invest well in looking after offspring. Conversely, in an insecure and unpredictable environment, the odds are in favour of entering puberty earlier and having offspring earlier, rather than banking on an uncertain future. To test this theory, one study in the USA first assessed attachment security at 15 months by categorizing the relationship with mother as either secure or insecure; and later assessed pubertal development up to 15 years. Of those classified as insecurely attached at 15 months, 43 per cent were considered early maturers; this compared to only 28 per cent of those who had been securely attached. Other studies have found that both stressful relationships with mothers and presence of a stepfather contribute to earlier pubertal maturation.

The secular trend in the age of puberty

Besides laying out the physical parameters of puberty, Tanner was the first to document what is called the secular trend in the age of puberty. This refers to changes through historical time. His analysis was on age of menarche, and for the earlier periods of time he made use of some records from the Scandinavian countries going back to the mid-19th century. In addition he used larger scale surveys in the USA, UK, and other European countries through the 20th century. The trends were clearly for a rather steady decrease of about 0.3 years per decade in the average age of menarche. This was from around 16 or 17 years at the start of records to around 13 years by the 1960s. Subsequently it was shown that some of the 19th century estimates were not reliable. Nevertheless the changes through the 20th century in the age of menarche, and also in the age of the growth spurt and the adult height attained, are well established. They have been found in other industrializing countries. For example, surveys in Beijing, China, found that the median age of girls at menarche decreased from around 14.9 in 1940 to 13.4 in the 1960s, 12.8 in 1980 and 12.1 in 2000.

The usually accepted explanation for this secular trend is that it is due to diet, nutrition, and general physical health. In the 19th century these were compromised in Western economies with the onset of the industrial revolution, and poor working conditions for those working in factories and manufacturing industries. But conditions improved through the 20th century. The secular trend shown by Tanner cannot be extrapolated too far backwards; the age of menarche in earlier centuries is very difficult to estimate, but in contemporary non-industrialized societies, while not usually as early as nowadays in Western societies (about 12–13 years) it is normally achieved by around 16 years. Also, the trend cannot be extrapolated too far forwards. Most of the evidence suggests a slowing down or cessation of the trend since the 1970s in the industrialized economies. For example, one study in North America found only a very small decline, from 12.9 years in 1948 to 12.8 years in 1992.

The impact of puberty

Puberty impacts on the development of the young person in a variety of ways. The most obvious are the *physical changes*. Entering puberty, the child becomes a young person. They will be aware of their growth spurt and associated changes in sexual development, which often leads to some awkwardness and self-consciousness. This can be compounded by their increased capacity for abstract thought (see Chapter 3) and social comparisons (see Chapter 4).

The way in which these physical changes impact on the young person will be affected by factors such as what they know and expect about puberty, and how puberty is viewed in their society. In many traditional societies, puberty is marked as a clear rite of passage, with rituals to mark when a girl has her first period or when a boy is considered no longer to be a child. These ceremonies change the status of the young person, and may help to move them from a primarily family-oriented network into a more grown-up peer-oriented network (Chapter 1). This latter aspect is particularly true for boys in some cultures.

In urban societies something similar may be found in some religious communities. For example in Orthodox Judaism, boys celebrate a Bar Mitzvah at 13 years (about the age of puberty in boys). They then take their place among the men in the synagogue. In liberal and reform Jewish congregations there is also a Bat Mitzvah for girls when they are 12 years of age. However most urban communities do not have such initiation ceremonies—then, how parents prepare their children for puberty and deal with it can make a difference. Some studies in the USA have suggested that the onset of menarche can be remembered as an unpleasant and troubling event, especially if the young person was not prepared for it and if they did not get much support from their mothers. Such negative aspects are more likely for early maturers. On the positive side, the shared experience of menarche and associated aspects of femininity can in some respects bring an adolescent girl and her mother closer.

The *growth hormones* and *sex hormones* are largely responsible for bringing about the physical changes in puberty. Do they also affect behaviours such as the mood swings often found in adolescence? This has certainly been a belief, which is often expressed in popular sayings about raging hormones. The emotional closeness that young people feel to parents does dip in adolescence (Chapter 4), and there is evidence that this is related to the onset of puberty—the dip in emotional closeness comes earlier for early maturers and later for late maturers. It is tempting to attribute this synchrony between puberty and emotional closeness to hormonal effects, however just the awareness of physical changes in the body may also play a part.

In fact the sex hormones, which surge as puberty approaches, are believed to cause changes in neural systems including parts of the brain. These effects have been divided into *organizational* and *activational*. Organizational changes affect the structure of the brain (through the number and branching of nerve cells), and indeed such effects of sex hormones are important in the prenatal and early infancy period in determining growth as a boy or girl; however there are further organizational effects around puberty.

An important organizational change at puberty is in the balance of what are called grey matter and white matter in the brain (so-called from their appearance, with grey matter being located more on the outer part of the brain, white matter more on the inside). Grey matter is mainly associated with processing information and cognition, and there is some decrease in this at adolescence related to what has been called *synaptic pruning*—a cutting back of less used material which despite some short-term effects will lead to more efficient neural growth in the longer term. By contrast there appears to be continuing growth of white matter, which is mainly myelinated (well-conducting) nerve fibres conveying messages to different areas of grey matter.

Activational changes refer to changes in the level of functioning of certain neural systems. There is evidence for effects of sex hormones on circadian rhythms and thus sleep patterns (Chapter 4) and on sensitivity to rewards and hence risk-taking behaviours (see Chapter 6). There is some evidence that hormone levels can affect moodiness and aggression, but these effects interact in a complex way with the changes in awareness and identity that occur around the same time (Chapter 3).

Brain development at adolescence

The hormonal effects on behaviour work through their effects on the brain, and over the last two decades changes in brain development around puberty have been studied quite extensively. This has been facilitated by progress in techniques to study brain activity, and linking this to behaviour. Neuroimaging techniques provide measures of brain processes, and one widely used method is functional magnetic resonance imaging (fMRI); here, blood oxygen levels in specific areas of the brain are assessed as a measure of brain activity. This can be related to specific stimuli or contexts. While many of these kinds of study relate to cognitive activities (a domain called cognitive neuroscience), some findings are also relevant to social behaviour, and a number of researchers have been writing about the social brain in adolescence.

The remodelling of the brain in adolescence has been related to a number of aspects of cognitive and social functioning. These include improvements in face processing (noticing and identifying faces), and identifying emotions in faces. The kind of emotion shown is important. One study found that recognition of fear improved steadily through childhood and adolescence, whereas recognition of anger improved sharply between adolescence and adulthood. Another study showed how emotional stimuli may grab the attention of adolescents more than adults. Using fMRI techniques, the attention paid by adolescents and adults to pictures of fearful and neutral faces, and the brain areas activated, were examined. Sometimes participants were asked to look at the emotional expressions in the pictures, but at other times they were asked to focus on a non-emotional aspect (such as nose width). Adolescents showed more brain activation in response to the emotional aspects of the stimuli, whereas adults were more able to activate the frontal cortex areas for the non-emotional task, while disregarding the emotions.

Other studies have suggested how brain development can affect games which involve trust and sharing. These behavioural economic games involve processes such as how two players agree to share some amount of money or tokens. In early adolescence, players tend to make more self-oriented choices; in later adolescence they consider the consequences for others more (Chapter 4). These changes have been related to changes in areas of the prefrontal cortex related to perspective-taking and impulse control.

Another area of research has related to peer influences. A particular interest has been in feelings about social rejection by peers (Chapters 4 and 6). Adolescents especially show greater distress at this kind of social exclusion, which has been related to activation in certain brain areas.

Research in these areas is progressing rapidly, but one proposal is for a dual systems model. The two systems change in different ways through adolescence. One system is of cognitive control, related to the increase in white matter and to prefrontal cortex development. Here connections increase, as do connections between cortical areas and subcortical areas such as the limbic system which are more involved with emotional responses. Thus, control over planning and emotions should increase rather steadily through the adolescent period. However a second system, a socioemotional system perhaps more related to hormonal influences and reward sensitivity, is linked to sensation seeking and related phenomena of adolescence described earlier. This increases quite rapidly going into puberty. Thus, according to this view, puberty brings about a temporary imbalance between emotional impulse and cognitive control. Figure 4 gives a very schematic view of this, showing how reward sensitivity moves

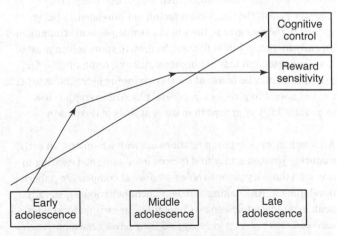

4. **Schematic representation of dual systems model.**

ahead of cognitive control for a time, in the early to middle adolescent period.

Consequences of early, on-time, and late puberty

As is shown in the Tanner diagrams in Figure 3, there can be considerable variation in the ages at which puberty is reached, even within one country at one historical period. But do these differences matter? What are the consequences for early or late maturers compared to those who are 'on-time' in their pubertal development? There has been considerable research on this, and the answers are different for boys and girls. A bottom line statement would be that early maturing boys may be at an advantage; whereas early maturing girls may not be. However the picture is complicated and depends on several factors.

One aspect of this relates to *body image* and *societal ideas of attractiveness*. We have seen how puberty changes the body in many ways. In some cultures and at some periods a thinner body image is idealized more for girls, such that early maturing girls may feel uncomfortable about their height and weight (see Chapter 7). Another important factor, not unrelated, is *being valued in the peer group*. Boys tend to value physical strength, and an early maturing boy will enter the growth spurt before most of his classmates and may get higher status as a result of this; for example he may be better at sports or winning fights. Such aspects are not absent in girls, but in general physical strength is less important in girls' groups than other aspects of reputation.

Although most peer group relations are with age-mates, an early maturing youngster may find it more interesting and exciting to mix with those a year or so older, who are at comparable pubertal development. Risk-taking and delinquent behaviours generally peak in middle adolescence (Chapter 5). An early maturer who *associates with older peers* may find themselves drawn into such activities earlier than they normally would be. Some research in

Sweden suggested that this effect can be particularly important for girls. In this study, many girls who reached puberty before 11 years did mix more with older peer groups, and those who did so also engaged in more norm-breaking activities such as taking drugs and truanting from school. Differences in norm-breaking activities were no longer found when the girls were followed up at 25 years, but some other differences were found. The early maturing girls engaged in sexual activity earlier, got married and had children earlier, and were less likely to be in higher education than late maturers. Interestingly, early maturing girls who did not associate with older peers did not show greater norm-breaking behaviours.

One influential theory, proposed by the American clinical psychologist Terrie Moffitt over twenty years ago, is that there is a *maturity gap* in adolescence between biological and social maturity. Such an approach is similar to the idea of *social adolescence* (Chapter 1), and is consistent with the work on hormones and brain development. But the theory has more to say than this. Firstly, the extent to which adolescents feel socially mature may depend on the kind of society they are in and what expectations are made of them. Do they have clearly defined roles and responsibilities, or are they in a *moratorium* whereby adults give them licence to explore new ways of behaving (see Chapter 3)? Secondly, Moffitt argued that the maturity gap will matter more if an adolescent is motivated to overcome it; if he or she accesses role models for risky behaviour (such as older peers); and if there is some reward for such behaviour. The maturity gap will be exaggerated for early maturers (and diminished for late maturers). Thus on this theory we would expect confirmation of the pattern found in the Swedish study mentioned earlier—that earlier maturers are more risky and become delinquent, especially when they mix with older peers. Other research has confirmed this pattern of findings, with late maturers sometimes found to be less at risk for norm-breaking behaviours. The pattern is relatively well-confirmed for girls, but for boys studies find that being either early or late can be a risk factor. However, early maturation does bring some clear benefits for boys.

Chapter 3
Formal operational thought, moral development, and identity

Cognitive development occurs all through childhood, and it is marked by advances in perceptual abilities, short- and long-term memory, ability to focus attention selectively, and reasoning abilities. Such advances continue in adolescence, generally but also in specific ways. For example, adolescents are on the whole much more capable than younger children of divided attention. They are able to do school work while listening to background music, or text friends while watching a TV programme. However, some particular aspects are thought to mark out adolescent cognition, notably *metacognition* (being able to think about your own thinking processes), *abstract reasoning*, and *hypothesis testing* (as in scientific reasoning). Following from this are the possibility of higher levels of moral reasoning; so-called *adolescent egocentrism*; and a quest for *identity*—reflecting on who you are and what you want to be. Three major theorists in these domains were Jean Piaget, Lawrence Kohlberg, and Erik Erikson.

Piaget and formal operational thinking

An influential and longstanding theory in cognitive development was proposed by Jean Piaget, a Swiss biologist and psychologist, during the 1930s to the 1950s. He described a stage model of cognitive development with abstract thought becoming possible by adolescence. A period he spent working in a psychiatric clinic led Piaget to become interested in psychoanalysis and clinical psychology as well as philosophy and epistemology. These interests and experiences, including a period working with Binet on the development of the earliest intelligence tests, led him to develop his own method of inquiry and theoretical framework to attempt to explain how our ways of thinking develop.

An important method that Piaget adopted was a form of *clinical interview*. This was not aimed at health problems, but at diagnosing the state of a child's or young person's mind. By asking questions in a conversational style, and probing what the child really understood about a problem, he aimed to find out what the child was capable of, and what was still beyond his or her cognitive reach. With younger children he also used observations, and sometimes he became a participant observer. He made a now-famous study of children's understanding of the game of marbles by watching how they played, discussed, and argued about the rules. He also joined in himself—even making mistakes to see how he would be corrected! However, with adolescents, he and his long-time collaborator Bärbel Inhelder made most use of small-scale experiments, generally on scientific reasoning type problems.

In his theoretical framework, Piaget argued that children and young people progress through a series of four stages in their cognitive abilities. These are the sensori-motor, pre-operational, concrete operational, and formal operational stages. The sensori-motor stage characterizes infancy (0–2 years) and finding out about basic properties of objects—such as that they continue to exist when out of sight; or that you can bang objects together to make sounds. In the pre-operational stage (around 2–7 years) children are learning about characteristics of objects such as colour, shape, and length; however, while understanding these terms, they will have difficulty in tasks such as classifying or sorting objects in more than one way (e.g. by shape and colour); arranging sticks in a series of ascending length (seriation); or understanding another's view of a three-dimensional scene. These sorts of tasks come to be fully understood in the concrete operational stage (around 7–12 years); children can now understand what are called the conservation tasks (e.g. that a sausage shape of Play-Doh rolled into a ball still has the same amount of material), and they can take the perspective of others in many situations. However, these abilities are, in the main, tied to the actual situations (objects, people) that the child is dealing with. Therefore these abilities or operations are called *concrete* rather than *abstract*.

The formal operational stage

Piaget saw the big advance of the final, formal operational stage as being a freeing up of cognitive abilities from the actual situation that you perceive as well as a systematic approach to testing ideas. In a simple form these can be seen in how certain abstract verbal tasks are tackled, such as syllogisms or letter combinations. As an example of a *syllogism*, consider the statements 'all black dogs have three heads', 'the next door neighbours have a black dog', and the question 'how many heads does it have?'. The concrete operational child is likely to get bogged down in arguing that no dog has three heads; the formal operational young person is more likely to accept the premises and reply 'three heads', ignoring the normal reality. *Letter combinations* are the sorts of puzzles often found in newspapers—for example, how many words can you make out of the letters A, E, F, R, and T. The concrete operational child can certainly have a go at this—after all the letters are in front of them, and maybe they will get ART and FAR and RAT. But here the difference is how the formal operational adolescent or adult is likely to go about the task. They will probably do it more systematically, thinking of how many words start with A, or T, etc., and what combinations of letters are possible—they will for example get AFTER and FEAR, and indeed all the possible words if they do a truly systematic search.

Inhelder and Piaget worked in Swiss schools with children and adolescents, using a number of scientific reasoning tasks. These included seeing what factors affected the time of swing of a pendulum; placing different weights on a plank around a fulcrum (lever point) to see what affects the balance; and predicting the effects of mixing different kinds of chemicals. Here the tasks are concrete in the sense of the materials actually being there, and younger children will have a go at this—but their attempts will be haphazard and unsystematic. The formal operational adolescent will go about things differently. They will be able to think abstractly, or in a hypothetical way, 'What if I tried this…' or 'If I do X then I can see if Y is true'. For example in the pendulum task, the young person is given strings of different lengths and weights of different heaviness. They attach a weight to a string, and they can also vary how far they pull the weight back before releasing it as a pendulum, and how forcefully they push it. The key to solving the task (what factors affect the time of swing?) is to vary one factor systematically, while holding the others constant (this will establish that the length of the string is the only important variable).

From these sorts of experiments, Inhelder and Piaget argued that young people characteristically became able to solve such tasks during the period of 11–15 years of age. Of course such abilities do not appear overnight, and they and subsequent theorists have distinguished substages: from early formal operations (some signs of abstract reasoning, but far from completely systematic) through to late formal operations (quite systematic approaches on a variety of tasks).

How Piaget's theory is seen today

For some decades after Inhelder and Piaget's work, and as Piaget's theory began to be more influential in English-speaking as well as French-speaking countries, researchers in the UK and USA carried out many replications and extensions of his work. By and large, the key changes exemplified by formal operational thinking have held up well. However, there developed considerable controversy about the timing, and the universality, of this fourth stage of thinking.

Regarding timing, it does seem that abstract and systematic thought becomes available in adolescence (and not much before). However, most evidence does not support Piaget's idea that it is normally achieved by 15 years. Studies during the 1970s found that formal operational thought continued developing through the adolescent period and indeed into adulthood. Typically, only a minority of 15-year-olds would be characterized as having fully achieved formal operations, even though they show some signs of it. Regarding universality, studies found considerable variation by domain (the actual kind of task involved, for example scientific, musical, linguistic), and by prior experience (such as extent of formal schooling).

In a reply to such criticisms in 1972, Piaget attempted a defence of his stage model for formal operational thought, but he had to make concessions. Regarding timing, he argued that normally all young people go through the stages, but at different speeds depending on the kinds of stimulation and experiences they have had. Regarding universality, he argued that aptitudes become more diversified with age, so that variation across domains will be found. He summarized that 'all normal subjects attain the stage of formal operations … if not between 11–12 to 14–15 years, in any case between 15 and 20 years. However, they reach this stage in different areas according to their aptitudes and professional specializations' (Piaget, *Intellectual evolution from adolescence to adulthood*, p. 10).

Much of Piaget's original writing can be heavy going, but this response is in one of his most accessible articles. However, it is only a partially successful defence, as if the stage is reached in different areas and at different ages by different persons, it is not such a strong universal stage of thinking as his earlier stages are. Research since then has focused more on domain specific abilities, suggesting that young people develop rules for certain kinds of problems that are specific to the kind of problem concerned. This gives a more gradual view of developing cognitive skills, rather than a general synchronized advance across all domains. Nevertheless the core aspects of formal operations (abstract thought and hypothetical reasoning) can be said to become available to adolescents, even if they are not universally achieved by them.

Piaget's work was primarily on physical objects and scientific reasoning tasks. But the advent of abstract and systematic thought has implications in more social domains, such as moral reasoning; the imaginary audience and personal fable; and thoughts about identity.

Kohlberg and moral reasoning

Moral reasoning refers to how children or young people reason about moral situations, including moral dilemmas. It is thus not so much about moral behaviour, but rather about the level of reasoning about it. The link between moral reasoning and moral behaviour is tenuous—a cruel person can often provide clever justifications for their behaviour.

The study of moral reasoning was pioneered by Lawrence Kohlberg in the USA. He first studied this by interviewing, every three years, a sample of fifty males aged 10–26. Kohlberg asked them questions about morality, such as 'why shouldn't you steal from a store?', and gave them hypothetical dilemmas to consider. The most well-known scenario concerns a man called Heinz whose wife is near death. Only an expensive drug can save her, but Heinz cannot afford the high price the druggist is charging. Eventually, when all else has failed, Heinz steals the drug in order to save his wife's life. Kohlberg asked whether he should have done this, and why. He was not interested in whether the respondent said 'yes' or 'no', but rather the kind of reasoning that was used to justify the answer.

Perhaps following Piaget's example, Kohlberg postulated a developmental stage model. He saw most pre-adolescent children as being at a level he called *preconventional morality*, where a situation is viewed basically in terms of what is good or bad for oneself—for example, it is wrong to steal from a store because you might get punished. However, Kohlberg argued that most adolescents advanced beyond this, to what he called *conventional morality*; here the young person takes the viewpoint of societal expectations—it is wrong to steal from a store because the law protects people's property, and if we do not obey the law then society will break down. Kohlberg also thought that some adults would reach a *postconventional morality*, but only after around age 20, and only in a minority of cases. Here someone judges the rules of society in terms of more general or abstract principles; thus it might be right to steal in certain circumstances, if a greater principle, such as saving a life, justifies it. Kohlberg linked these developments to Piaget's stages. He thought that conventional morality corresponded to early formal operational thinking, while postconventional morality would only be possible for those who have achieved late formal operational thinking. Thus, we might regard adolescents as normally moving into the level of moral reasoning that most adults engage in.

A number of researchers have developed Kohlberg's ideas, in some cases using more realistic dilemmas that might occur naturally in their lives—for example about trust, sharing, and conflict in peer groups. Similar stages have been found in many countries as regards the preconventional and conventional levels. The postconventional level has been argued to be more culturally specific. For example, cultures have been characterized as more individualistic (e.g. USA, western Europe) or collectivist (many Eastern and/or more traditional societies). Judging one's society by one's own moral principles could be seen as a typically individualistic way of thinking, and thus not to be so expected in collectivistic societies.

Kohlberg's original study, and his stages, were based only on males. Carol Gilligan described a study involving women aged 15–33 and how they reasoned about abortion. This was a very real issue for them, as they were all pregnant and attending abortion- and pregnancy-counselling services. Gilligan argued that any postconventional stage in these women was not based on universal abstract principles, but rather on the impact of decisions on people's feelings and well-being. She called this a responsibility rather than a justice orientation.

Imaginary audience and personal fable

The ability to think in abstract and hypothetical ways has been argued to affect adolescents in other ways. One way of being affected may be an increased preoccupation with imagining how others think of your appearance, such as your body shape, clothes, or hair style. A study in the USA found that girls (but not boys) experienced increased dissatisfaction with their bodies over the period 13–18 years; this dissatisfaction was only weakly related to how other adolescents rated their physical attractiveness. Such preoccupations are likely to be amplified by the bodily changes at puberty (Chapter 2) and the increased influence of the peer group (Chapter 4); they can lead to an increased incidence of problems such as anorexia and bulimia (Chapter 7). David Elkind summed up this kind of preoccupation in the expression *imaginary audience*. We probably all sometimes think while getting dressed in the morning, 'Shall I wear these clothes?', 'Are they appropriate?', 'How will they seem to others?', but for adolescents these questions could be a rather constant and important concern, in a way that has become possible with the development of formal operational thinking.

Elkind also coined the concept of *personal fable*. This is an imaginary story or even a fantasy of what your life will be—you could be a pop star, a great writer, a leading politician. This is the kind of thinking that most of us engage in from time to time, but

Elkind argued it is particularly characteristic of adolescents, especially as their identity is usually still to be fully formed.

Some research has suggested that the imaginary audience and personal fable phenomena do indeed peak during adolescence, and are to some extent linked to stages in formal operational thought. Similar to the imaginary audience, adolescents become increasingly aware of other's perspectives, as well as developing their own identity, leading to greater self-consciousness and awareness of how others may evaluate them (Chapter 4). Elkind talked generally about these phenomena as being examples of *adolescent egocentrism*, a preoccupation with oneself, but different from childhood egocentrism (an inability to take the other person's point of view).

Erikson and the development of identity

The onset of sexual maturity at puberty and the increased self-awareness and ability for abstract thought coming at adolescence mean that the young person is both able and often impelled to think about what sort of person they are and want to become. This is also affected by societal rules (e.g. choices on whether and how to continue schooling; the right to vote; the right to fight in the armed forces) and expectations (e.g. whether adolescence is seen and tolerated as a period of experimentation).

This search for identity was proposed as a key aspect of adolescence by Erik Erikson. Based on extensive clinical practice, Erikson proposed eight developmental stages through the lifespan, each of which had a *normative crisis*. This was an area of major challenge which needed to be overcome successfully if the person was to move forward in a psychologically healthy way. Erikson thought that the normative crisis for adolescence was *identity vs. role confusion*. This is often referred to as an *identity crisis* at adolescence.

Erikson devoted much attention to the adolescent stage, and he wrote a book on the topic, *Identity: Youth and Crisis*, in 1968. The crisis aspect was perhaps pointed up here because the 1960s saw the Vietnam War, and massive protests by students and young people in the USA and other Western countries. Also, Erikson may have had a deep personal interest in identity, as he was brought up by his mother and step-father, and never knew who his biological father was. Nevertheless, his ideas caught on and have formed the basis of much later research.

Although still influential, some implications of the identity crisis have been challenged. One observation is that changes can be quite gradual and over a number of years, rather than a sudden 'crisis' being experienced. Also, adolescents typically experience challenges in various domains at different times. For example they need to start thinking about sexual behaviour and attitudes to this once they are sexually mature (early adolescence), whereas the possibility of voting for a particular political party may be at a later age (later adolescence). Finally, while adolescence may be an important time for facing identity issues, such concerns can often happen in later life; for example married women may go through such identity issues as they have children, and again as their children grow up and start schooling themselves.

Another important concept that came from Erikson's writings is the *psychosocial moratorium*. This is as much about societal expectations as about young people themselves. The idea is that while an adolescent is going through the identity crisis, or at least actively thinking about aspects of their identity, they explore or try out different possibilities. This is tolerated by parents and other adults. For example, an adolescent might try out religious or political beliefs that differ from those of their parents; or they may dress in unusual ways. The moratorium concept supposes that these will be relatively tolerated during adolescence, since it is understood that this is a period of exploration and the young person will settle on a more secure and stable identity in due course. While the moratorium concept has had some appeal, it does seem somewhat historically and culturally limited compared with the more general concept of a search for identity. Many societies have clear role expectations, even for young people, such that any moratorium would be difficult to detect.

The measurement of identity status

Erikson was more of a theorist than empirical investigator. His ideas needed to be operationalized and tested. This was done by James Marcia, who developed an interview schedule to ask about a young person's thoughts and beliefs regarding occupation, religion, political belief, and attitudes to sexual behaviour. Marcia was interested in whether the person showed *exploration* and *commitment*. Depending on the possible combinations of exploration and commitment, he classified someone, based on their responses, into one of four identity status types: *diffusion* (or *confusion*), *foreclosure*, *moratorium*, or *identity achievement*. Some typical responses for each type (to a question on occupation) are shown in Table 2.

Diffusion status would characterize children or younger adolescents who have not yet entered into the search for identity in that domain. Foreclosure status refers to someone who has made a commitment, but without going through any challenge or search process—maybe just accepting family or societal expectations without questioning them. Moratorium status refers to someone going through the challenge or crisis; they are actively thinking about the issues and trying out alternatives, either in real life or abstractly in their mind. Achievement refers to someone who has been through the exploration and challenge, and has consolidated their identity in this domain.

Marcia's identity statuses proved useful in later research. Identity achievement does increase by later adolescence, and longitudinal research does suggest some transitions from diffusion or

Table 2. Types of identity status illustrated by typical answers

IDENTITY STATUS	Typical response to: 'Have you decided what occupation you want to go in to?'
DIFFUSION (D) (neither exploration nor commitment)	'No, I haven't really thought much about that yet.'
FORECLOSURE (F) (commitment but no exploration)	'My dad is a miner so I'm expected to do the same.'
PSYCHOSOCIAL MORATORIUM (M) (exploration but no commitment)	'I'm not sure—I had thought of being a journalist but now I'm wondering about becoming a biologist.'
IDENTITY ACHIEVEMENT (A) (both exploration and commitment)	'Yes, I'm going to university to study medicine and be a doctor. I thought about it a lot and did some voluntary work at the local hospital and now I'm sure it's what I want to do.'

foreclosure, through moratorium to achievement. However, later research has differentiated Marcia's two concepts of exploration and commitment. Exploration has been described as being either in breadth or in depth. Exploration in breadth refers to comparing a variety of possibilities before making a choice (e.g. looking carefully at all the political party manifestos before deciding how to vote); exploration in depth means reflecting on one's current commitments (perhaps, wondering if you were right to vote for the party that you chose). Some studies have found that early adolescence is more characterized by exploration in breadth and moving to some choice or commitment; whereas later adolescence is more characterized by exploration in depth, with a possible re-evaluation of an earlier choice. This suggests some movement to-and-fro between moratorium (M) and achievement (A)—a process called a *MAMA cycle* (Figure 5).

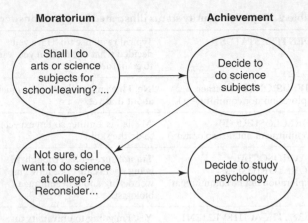

Moratorium **Achievement**

Shall I do arts or science subjects for school-leaving? ... → Decide to do science subjects

Not sure, do I want to do science at college? Reconsider... → Decide to study psychology

5. A hypothetical MAMA cycle.

Studying these processes needs longitudinal research, and some more recent studies have examined how identity changes over periods of months, or even on a day-to-day basis.

Identity and adjustment

One study in later adolescence, of Dutch students, looked at changes over six months in six domains: philosophy of life, parents, friends, studies, self, and intimate relationships. The patterns of change over six months varied considerably by domain, but many students were either stable or showed a moratorium to achievement or MA trajectory. Students with stable commitment (some in A, but also some in foreclosure, F) showed greatest levels of well-being. Another study looked at day-to-day variations. Fluctuations on a daily basis were taken as a sign of weaker identity commitment; and greater fluctuations predicted increases in internalizing symptoms such as depression. This suggests that some form of commitment is an important aspect of well-being as the young person moves through the adolescent period.

Many studies have found that internalizing symptoms are fewer in the higher commitment statuses (A and F) and greater for those in M. If you are confident of your identity, you are less likely to be depressed. But what about externalizing (aggressive, delinquent) behaviours? Another study of Dutch adolescents studied identity formation from 14 to 18 years, relating this to teacher ratings of externalizing problems at 11–12 years. They found that those at risk of earlier externalizing behaviours showed less identity commitment; they were more likely to be engaged in in-depth exploration, or in *searching moratorium*, meaning they were going back to revise commitments already reached (as in the MAMA cycle). This and related studies have suggested a reciprocal relationship between externalizing problems and difficulty in achieving a stable identity.

Another aspect of identity is what has been called ethnic and racial identity (ERI). This can embrace a number of aspects, including how thoroughly a person identifies with a particular ethnic or racial group; how important this is for them; how they evaluate their group; and how they perceive others to evaluate their group. A review in the USA of different minority ethnic groups (African American; Latino; Asian American / Pacific Islander; and Native American) related ERI to different areas of adjustment. Many aspects of ERI were positively associated with psychosocial functioning (self-esteem, internalizing symptoms). There was even stronger or more consistent evidence linking ERI to better academic outcomes. However, looking at health risk behaviours (such as illegal drug use, unprotected sex), more mixed findings were obtained. This might be because such risky behaviours have different meaning for different groups, and indeed may not be as undesirable for adolescents themselves as adults often believe (Chapter 6).

Chapter 4
Relationship changes—parents and peers

Adolescence is a period of great change in relationships with parents as well as with peers. A traditional, simple view was that relationships with peers became more influential, and relationships with parents less so, through the teenage years. This has some truth in it; the young person is becoming increasingly independent from parents and spending more time in peer groups through the teenage years. However, the picture is inevitably complex, and varies in different cultural settings and historical periods.

Parents

One change in relationship with parents is in general emotional closeness. This was well documented in a study in the USA, which reported ratings for how close young people felt to parents, at ages 10, 16, and 25. The findings showed clearly that teenagers did not rate themselves as close to parents as did preteens or young adults. Ratings for closeness to mothers were higher than for closeness to fathers, but for both parents there was a dip in closeness at 16 years, by about 1 or 1.5 points on a 7 point scale. An interesting aspect of this study was an additional historical dimension. There was data for two birth cohorts: one set of data for people born in 1925–39 (who were adolescents in the 1940s–50s) and a second for people born during 1950–9 (who were adolescents in the 1960s–70s). The dip in closeness was greater for the latter cohort, perhaps because compared to the 1940s and 1950s, the 1960s were notable for social protest around the Vietnam War in which young people played a prominent role.

This distancing from parents should not be over-exaggerated. In this study, mean ratings of closeness did remain positive. It found that most adolescents maintain good relationships with parents most of the time, and still use them as sources of emotional support and advice. Nevertheless the changes during this period are real, and can be strongly experienced by many parents. These changes can be related to the coming of puberty, as they appear to be more closely related to pubertal timing than chronological age. They are also related to the brain changes at this time and to the cognitive changes, especially the search for identity and autonomy. Indicators of these changes include issues around trust and disclosure; and parent–adolescent conflicts.

Trust and disclosure

How much do young people trust in their parents such that they are willing to disclose their worries and concerns, and take or seek advice? A common distinction made here is between *prudential* concerns and *personal* concerns. Prudential concerns relate to risky behaviours such as taking drugs or talking to strangers on the internet. Personal concerns relate to normally non-risky choices such as choice of friends or how to spend one's leisure time. When asked, adolescents typically say that they ought to talk to their parents about prudential concerns, whereas talking about personal concerns is not seen as so necessary. But their actual behaviour often does not correspond to what they feel they ought to do. They disclose less about their prudential concerns, because they are afraid of disapproval, punishment, or sanctions. They will try to avoid lying to parents, but to avoid full disclosure of risky activities they may use strategies such as avoiding the issue, only telling if asked directly, and leaving out important details.

One study compared these findings, many from studies in the USA, with behaviour of adolescents aged around 16 years in Japan. A very similar pattern was found. Adolescents felt more obligation to disclose prudential issues (in Japan, these included drinking sake and going to arcade centres), but actually disclosed these less often than they did personal issues about which they felt less obligation. Although the structure of findings was quite similar, actual rates of disclosure and of obligation to disclose were noticeably lower in Japanese than in US adolescents, perhaps because of a greater concern to avoid disrupting family harmony in Japanese culture.

Parent–adolescent conflicts

Another manifestation of parent–child distancing is an increase in conflicts. One review suggested that the frequency of conflicts is highest in early adolescence, while their intensity is highest in the mid-adolescent years. A number of studies have been made about what such conflicts are about. For example, a study of 11–14-year-old African-American adolescents in the USA found the most frequent conflicts were about doing domestic chores (21 per cent), choice of activities (17 per cent), or issues of interpersonal relationships such as choice of friends (17 per cent), followed by the state of the adolescent's room (13 per cent), schoolwork (10 per cent), time for going to bed (9 per cent), appearance (6 per cent), and money (5 per cent). A similar study was later made of 11–18-year-olds in Hong Kong, and in Shenzhen, China (a mainland Chinese city bordering Hong Kong). In both sites, the traditional Chinese socialization pattern places more emphasis on family obligations and responsibility to elders than is usually the case in Western countries. However, many conflicts were again about choice or regulation of activities (using the phone, watching TV, bedtimes), and doing household chores. Some conflicts were also about money and looks/health. In Shenzhen there were more conflicts over achievement (studying, homework), with a greater emphasis on the importance of good school grades; there were fewer interpersonal conflicts over relationships with parents, siblings, and friends, perhaps because most of the adolescents were in one-child families and had no siblings to quarrel with.

These studies used interviews with a large number of young people to ask about conflicts. In a different kind of approach, researchers in the Netherlands carried out an intensive study with just seventeen girls, over one year. They were 15 years old when the study started, and they were asked to keep a diary record of conflicts with their mothers. They did this for two-week periods, every six weeks. They could record the conflicts online or written in a booklet, and they got a small reward for each completed week. The researchers first classified the total of 147 conflicts recorded into five main types: autonomy (e.g. when to go to bed, when to do homework; 51 per cent); not like me (a discrepancy between how the girl saw herself and how she was seen and reacted to by her mother; 20 per cent); dependency (the daughter wanting help or advice from the mother; 13 per cent); unfairness (the daughter feels she is treated unfairly; 9 per cent); and minor-scope conflicts (e.g. brushing hair painfully, losing a sandwich box; 7 per cent). These conflicts generated a range of emotional responses, such as feeling angry, frustrated, ashamed, misunderstood, not taken seriously. Generally, those girls who had more conflicts over the year reported more different emotional states. But the researchers found that for a small number of girls who reported the most conflicts, this was not true. These girls reported conflicts in a range of different areas, but with the same associated emotional state. These girls and their mothers appeared caught in a rigid pattern of re-enacting the same kind of conflicts, with the same outcomes, throughout the year. For most of the girls, though, there was much more variability and flexibility.

Autonomy and control

In studies around conflict, it appears that parents often see the issues as being matters of social convention. As one mother stated: 'I think it is important for him to see that everybody participates in the household tasks. Because if he didn't have to do it, somebody else has to, and generally it's me'. However, adolescents themselves seem to view these conflicts as being about issues of personal autonomy, in opposition to attempts at parental control. They were seeking to develop their own rights in decision-making, rather than automatically give way to parents' wishes. Thus, even though many conflicts are about mundane matters, they may contribute to a decrease in parent–child closeness if parents resist this bid for autonomy. A study of Asian-American adolescents in the USA found that in families where parents did allow an earlier timetable of autonomy, adolescents reported greater closeness to parents, and higher self-esteem.

Some studies have distinguished three kinds of parental control, as indicated in Table 3. These can have very different consequences for adolescent development. One longitudinal study looked at use of these kinds of parental control and the psychological functioning of adolescents aged 12–13 years, over a six-month period. This was done in two sites: Chicago, USA, and Beijing, China. Many findings were similar in the USA and China (Table 3). *Psychological control* predicted decreases in emotional well-being. *Psychological autonomy support* predicted gains for both emotional well-being and academic achievement; this being a noticeably stronger effect in the USA than in China. *Behavioural control* predicted gains in academic achievement. Overall, parents decreased their attempts to control adolescents' personal decisions through the early adolescent years in both countries, but noticeably more so in the USA. Furthermore, in both countries a greater decrease in parental control was associated with better adolescent emotional well-being; but again this effect was much

Table 3. Types of parental control and their possible long-term effects

Type of parental control	Examples	Possible long-term effects
Psychological control	Guilt induction, love withdrawal, and authority assertion	Negative effects over time on emotional well-being
Psychological autonomy support	Facilitating choices, opinion exchange	Positive effects over time for both emotional well-being and academic achievement
Behavioural control	Talking about free time activities, having rules about time out	Positive effects over time for academic achievement

more noticeable in the USA, perhaps because such a decrease is more normative in Western culture and more expected by the young person as a result.

These studies suggest that parents of adolescents have a fine line to tread—some rules are important, but discussion and flexibility that acknowledges the young person's own feelings and desires is also necessary. One area where some parent–adolescent conflict is often difficult to avoid is around adolescent bedtimes.

Adolescent bedtimes

Sleep patterns change through adolescence in two important ways. First is what has been called *delayed phase preference*: teenagers go to bed later and get up later in the morning, especially at weekends. This has been argued to be a natural consequence of the biological changes associated with puberty. A pacemaker in the hypothalamus maintains a state of alertness later into the evening than was the case in childhood, a trend that starts to reverse again in early adulthood. A second change is part of a more continuous trend from infancy onwards and through adulthood of a decrease in sleep duration. Nevertheless adolescents still need more sleep than adults, and the late bedtimes means that they often get less sleep than they need.

Paul Kelley, a researcher who was previously a head teacher at a high school in northern England, has argued that adult schedules are unresponsive to the changes in sleep patterns that adolescents are going through. The result of normal school start times of 9 am is that adolescents are typically sleep deprived, with adverse consequences for learning, grumpiness at school in the morning, and increased likelihood of conflicts with teachers. While a head teacher, he tried out the effect of starting school at 10 am and reported very positive outcomes, both academic and in terms of the atmosphere in the school changing for the better. A larger scale project is now assessing whether this finding can be replicated in a large sample of schools.

Family and school

The research on bedtimes illustrates how family practices can impact on life in school. One study in the USA used daily diary data over a two-week period to examine this. Parents and adolescents (aged around 15 years) reported on conflicts, and adolescents also reported on daily mood and school problems (such as being late or getting a bad grade). Conflict between parents and adolescents predicted school problems on the same day and up to two days later. Vice versa, school problems predicted conflicts at home. Interestingly, parent–parent conflict did not predict school problems, at least not within the time scale of this study; the effect was limited to conflict with the adolescents themselves. Negative mood reported by the adolescents seemed to account for much of what the authors called a 'spillover effect' between home and school.

The peer group

As adolescents become independent from their parents, they spend more time with peers, and turn to peers more frequently for social support and identity. This starts with same-sex peers but increasingly involves opposite-sex peers later in adolescence. A classic study of Australian adolescents and young people aged 13–21 years used a combination of observations, questionnaires, diaries, and interviews to document this. In early adolescence, many teenagers went around with some three to nine individuals of the same sex; they interacted little outside their own clique. But a few years later they would be in larger groups or crowds, made up of several interacting cliques. These would still be same-sex groups, but the more mature or higher status members would start to make contact with members of the opposite sex. Gradually, other members of the crowd would follow their lead. This led to a stage where heterosexual crowds were made up of male and female cliques in loose association. After this, romantic relationships developed (Chapter 8).

A more recent study in the USA confirmed these trends, using a combination of questionnaires and telephone interviews to ask children and young people how much time they spent with peers, from middle childhood (8 years) into late adolescence (18 years). The time spent with same-sex peers increased steadily from 8 to 14 years. After this it started to decline, as more time began to be spent with opposite-sex peers. Time spent with opposite-sex peers increased after puberty (so, earlier for girls than boys), overtaking time spent with same-sex peers later in adolescence.

These researchers also assessed problem behaviours (drinking alcohol, smoking, skipping school), depressive symptoms, social competence, and school performance. Over time, more supervised time with peers (when an adult or older person was present) correlated with improved academic performance, while more unsupervised time with peers predicted greater problem behaviours and depressive symptoms, perhaps because of the influence of older peers.

Peer friendships

Peer friendships are different from relationships with parents or caregivers. The parent relationship is often characterized as one of *unilateral authority*, whereas friendship with peers is characterized as *mutual and reciprocal*. Divergent opinions may be expressed and new ideas discussed. While parent–child relations may become more mutual during adolescence, they do not become as truly mutual or reciprocal as peer relationships.

In early and middle childhood, friendship is described by children themselves as playing together and helping each other. This conception deepens in adolescence with an understanding that friends show intimacy and mutuality in a relationship that continues despite minor setbacks. A commonly used measure of quality of friendship assesses four positive elements: Companionship, Help, Security, and Closeness. There is more intense social activity between friends, and also more frequent conflict resolution (part of the Security measure); friends may quarrel, but they get over quarrels more effectively than non-friends do.

A number of studies have used behavioural economic games to examine trust and sharing between peers. For example, in the Ultimatum Game, two players are given a sum of money: player 1 has to decide on how to split this, and player 2 has the option of accepting this or declining (in which case neither gets any money). Fairness in this increases through childhood and adolescence, and has been related to mentalizing abilities. In the Trust Game, again two players have a sum of money to share. Here, player 1 can either decide on a split or to trust player 2 to decide the split, in which case the amount of money is tripled. This is a one-off game, so although letting player 2 decide could be very advantageous, it does require player 1 to trust player 2 to give him or her a fair share. In early adolescence, players tend to make more self-oriented choices; in later adolescence they consider the consequences for others more. They also tend to be more discriminating, being more prosocial with friends. Some of these changes have been related to shifts in activity in the social brain areas (Chapter 1).

The nature of friendships has been affected in recent years by the prevalent use of the internet and social networking sites (Chapter 5). Young people can have very many 'friends' on Facebook, for example, including both those familiar offline but also those only known online. Discussion on the nature of online friends has contrasted two positions. The *displacement hypothesis* argues that online friendships, being both much more numerous and often lacking direct physical contact, are basically more superficial; they are displacing traditional offline friendships but do not have their qualities such as intimacy and support. By contrast, the *stimulation hypothesis* argues that online friendships can supplement the quality and quantity of communication, leading to increased intimacy and support.

At present, the evidence is thought to be more in favour of the stimulation hypothesis. Existing offline friends can communicate more often by going online, and generally this facilitates closeness. Some young people who might be awkward in face-to-face interactions may find it easier initially to share information and develop some intimacy with peers while online. Nevertheless, this is a rapidly changing situation, as internet penetration increases to younger ages, and the nature and opportunities provided by social networking sites continue to evolve.

Popularity issues

The structure of friendships and position in the peer group have been studied using sociometric techniques. This can be done by observation, but is more usually done by asking children who their friends are, or who they like most and like least, in their class or peer group. For adolescents, besides asking for friendship nominations, researchers may ask questions like, 'Are there people who hang around together a lot at school? Who are they?' in order to look at the structure of larger cliques and gangs. By combining information from different informants, it is possible to develop a *social-cognitive map* of the peer group structure in adolescents. Besides looking at the position of an individual in the group, it is also possible to look at the centrality of a group or clique in the wider peer group network of the school.

Those who are at the centre of a social group and have many friends are described as popular. But in fact researchers have described two kinds of peer popularity. *Sociometric popularity* is having many friends and not being disliked by many others. Typically, a popular teenager will get many nominations as liked most and few if any as liked least when classmates are questioned. Sociometrically popular children are usually cooperative, well-adjusted, and confident. Another kind of popularity is called *perceived popularity*. This is a measure of social visibility obtained by asking classmates not who they actually like, but rather who they think are the most popular students.

There is an overlap between these two measures, but actually quite a limited one. Those who are high on both sociometric popularity and perceived popularity are generally prosocial and socially skilled, but not overly aggressive. However, others who are just high on perceived popularity may be sociometrically controversial. This means they get a lot of liked most but also a lot of liked least nominations. They are likely to be in a high status group or clique, but quite possibly one that is rather dominating, aggressive, or bullying. Some research suggests that this may be more common in girls than in boys. A study in the USA asked 8th grade adolescents to describe what it meant to be popular. Being cool was the most common response. However, more boys mentioned being athletic and funny. More girls mentioned being attractive, but also being mean, snobby, and rude; these latter are characteristics of relational aggression which appear to be more related to perceived popularity in girls.

Changes in peer influence

At any age there is a tendency to conform to significant others—to go along with what your friends think or do. Is this stronger in adolescence? Some evidence has suggested that conformity with peers increases up to around 14 years before declining again, perhaps especially so far as antisocial behaviours are concerned. However, there are conflicting views on this.

One view emphasizes *peer evaluation* and *fear of rejection*. Anxieties about friendships with peers peak in mid-adolescence. One study asked adolescents to complete unfinished sentences about friendships in a small group, and analysed the results for their emotional content. Themes of anxiety and fear of rejection by friends increased from 11 to 13 and then to 15 years, but declined by 17 years. A similar finding has been made regarding feelings about social rejection or ostracism by peers. This research has used a laboratory paradigm called *Cyberball*. Cyberball is an internet ball-passing game in which the young person thinks they are playing with two other players (in fact the other players are controlled by computer algorithms so as to include or exclude the participant). Mood and anxiety following exclusion are assessed. One study compared young adolescents (11–13 years), mid-adolescents (14–15 years), and adults (22–47 years) playing this game. The adolescents showed greater distress at social exclusion in the game, with anxiety being raised most noticeably in the young adolescent group. In a related paradigm, adolescent girls showed greater social anxiety to peer evaluation, related to activation of brain areas concerned with processing emotions.

An alternative viewpoint is that part of the cognitive and social development of adolescence is an increase in *autonomy* and *maturity*. This might imply that peer influence could be resisted if it went against one's own values. Some researchers constructed a measure of Resistance to Peer Influence (RPI), which included items such as 'Some people go along with their friends just to keep their friends happy, BUT other people refuse to go along with their friends just to keep their friends happy', with the respondent asked how true this is of them. They found a general increase in RPI with age from 9 through to mid-20s, and especially from 14 to 18 years (although there does appear to be a small dip at 14 years). Girls scored higher on RPI than boys.

Overall, it seems likely that through adolescence there is an increasing potential for autonomy and resistance to peer influence, but that nevertheless the influence of the peer group is very considerable, and fears of peer group rejection are high, especially in early adolescence.

Aggression and bullying

A more negative side of peer relationships is found when a young person is ignored or rejected by others. Social exclusion, as well as more active attempts to damage someone's social standing in a group or their friendships, perhaps by nasty rumour spreading, is seen as a form of aggression called *relational aggression*. Aggression is usually defined as behaviour intended to hurt another, and traditionally it has been seen as physical or verbal. Of course physical and verbal kinds of aggression occur in adolescence, but relational aggression is also common, and relatively more so than in early or middle childhood. It is a more sophisticated kind of aggression; it is less obvious to adults, and it can be justified by those doing it in terms of personal choice of friends or sharing information about others.

Some level of aggressive behaviour can be seen as normative and indeed part of growing up. It is something to be coped with throughout life. However, *bullying* is a kind of aggressive behaviour that raises special concerns. Bullying is normally defined as repeated aggressive behaviour with an imbalance of power. The victim, because they are physically or psychologically weaker in some way, cannot readily defend themselves. Those particularly at risk of being bullied in school include young people lacking good friends; who are shy or unassertive; or who have some kind of disability. Racial and sexual harassment can also be seen as forms of bullying. Sexual harassment often involves girls as victims, from other girls or boys, often involving appearance or reputation. This could be offline but now increasingly may be online (Chapter 5). Boys may also be at risk of such relational bullying, but usually in terms of derogatory comments about supposed or actual sexual orientation. Such homophobic bullying can affect girls as well, but usually appears more prevalent and severe for boys.

How young people cope with being bullied varies, but seeking help is generally a good strategy. Unfortunately, readiness to seek help from teachers or parents is much less in adolescence than in earlier childhood. Peer support schemes (in which trained pupils may offer mentoring or counselling) may provide an alternative route for getting support, at least initially. Over the last twenty years awareness of school bullying and its effects has greatly increased. Many schools now have anti-bullying policies (a legal requirement in some countries) and take active steps to reduce or deal with bullying, including curriculum work, restorative approaches, and graded sanctions.

Chapter 5
Youth culture—leisure pursuits and the cyberworld

Adolescents spend a great deal of time in leisure pursuits. Some of these are traditional, such as hanging out with friends, playing sports and games, and playing or making music. Since the 1950s, television viewing has taken up much leisure time, and a generation later computer games became popular. All these remain common leisure activities, but this century has also seen a massive change through information and communication technologies (ICT): mobile phones, and then smart phones, as well as desktop and laptop computers and tablets for accessing the internet. At the time of writing, social networking sites (SNS) play a major part in teenagers' lives (Figure 6), and trends in internet use continue to change rapidly.

Leisure activities are not just recreational but can have an important role in identity formation and in becoming a part of youth culture. Some of these leisure activities, such as watching TV, can be rather passive activities. However, advocates of *positive youth development* argue that leisure activities such as sports, arts, hobbies, and clubs are especially important in modern Western societies. This is because adolescents typically lack the roles and responsibilities that are often found in traditional societies, and suitable leisure activities can develop initiative and self-esteem.

6. Entering adolescence, this 12-year-old already has many friends on Facebook.

Reed Larson has argued that two important aspects of activities are *intrinsic motivation* (the young person must want to take part) and *concerted engagement* (concentration in order to meet some challenge in the activity). An activity that features both intrinsic motivation and concentrated engagement will be most valuable developmentally. In work in the USA he asked high school students about 15 years old to rate their psychological state regarding these two aspects in four contexts: in class; with friends; during sports; and doing arts and hobbies. Both sports activities, and arts and hobbies, scored high on both aspects. Classwork in school needed concentration but for most pupils it did not score highly on motivation. By contrast, hanging around with friends was motivating but usually did not require much concentration or challenge.

Sports activities

Participation in sports is a major interest amongst adolescents. This can be informal, but is often through after-school clubs or sports programmes. In the US, the most popular for boys are football, basketball, athletics, and baseball; and, for girls, basketball, athletics, volleyball, and softball. According to the Youth Risk Behavior Surveillance (YRBS) 2013 survey across the USA, nearly 60 per cent of males and 49 per cent of females in grades 9–14 (about 14–18 years) had engaged in at least one team sport in the previous twelve months.

Organized sports programmes are often seen as a means of enhancing adolescent development in ways which are approved of by adults, but that are also naturally enjoyed by young people themselves. There are obvious physical benefits to the vigorous exercise which most sports entail, but it is also thought that participation in sports can help develop aspects of identity, self-esteem, and confidence. Life skills which can be practised in many team-based sports include goal setting, communicating effectively, problem-solving, dealing with conflict, managing emotions, providing and receiving feedback, accepting interdependence, appreciating differences, and managing time and stress.

However, there can be negative as well as positive aspects to sport participation, and it does depend on how such programmes are experienced and managed. An individual adolescent will be comparing his or her performance and abilities to those of peers, and such social comparison processes will not always lead to greater self-esteem. Most of us will have embarrassing memories of missing the crucial goal or not being picked for the top team. Much depends on how such disappointments are coped with. Here the role of the coach or adult supervisor can be very important. A good coach can provide a model of leadership but also of social support in overcoming difficulties and failure. A poor coach might make such experiences worse. This implies that training for coaches should encompass these kinds of psychological aspects alongside the obvious training in the skills of the particular sport.

Television use

First introduced widely in the 1950s, watching television programmes continues to be a popular activity, although declining recently with the increasing use of the internet and social networking sites. Much television watching is purely for entertainment or excitement, but it can also be informative. The decades from the 1960s to 1990s saw most interest in researching the effects of TV viewing. Areas of concern then were surrounding issues of stereotyping and aggression.

Gender stereotypes in television programmes are reflected in the relative numbers of male and female characters, with males usually predominating. However, beyond that, stereotypes can be seen in the ways in which male and female roles are presented. Male roles are often more powerful; female roles more subservient or less important. Similarly, portrayals of different racial or ethnic groups may be unbalanced. In the US, the proportion of African-Americans on television programmes watched by children was actually found to be higher than the proportion in the population, but the proportions of other ethnic groups (Latino, Asian American, and Native American) were much lower than those found in the general population. Compared to White Americans, other groups may be portrayed negatively in terms of status, behaviour, and achievement. Awareness of the need to give more balanced portrayals is increasing, but issues around stereotypes also apply to other media including those accessed through the internet.

Another prominent concern about some television programmes has been the extent of overt aggression portrayed. Again, such concerns can also apply to other media, especially, in this case, to violent computer games. In these media, violence can be glamorized or trivialized. Defenders of such violence will argue that it is clearly distinguished from reality and that the exciting emotional experiences engendered can be cathartic. Critics say that such arousal will associate aggression with positive feelings, that young people may become desensitized to violence, and that violent actions seen on the media may be imitated in real life.

Some longitudinal studies have looked at long-term effects from childhood into adolescence, and although the findings are not always clear-cut, many researchers feel that aggression on television or other media does result in increased levels of real life aggression. We also know from case studies that media violence can on occasion provide a stimulus or model for some violent crime. But it may be that for most young people, most of the time, the impact of television is rather small. Any influence of violence on television needs to be considered in the context of other, non-media factors. For example, actual aggression in the home between parents or with siblings is not as easily turned off as a television set, and might be a more powerful influence than fictitious aggression on the media.

Use of ICT

The tremendous increase in penetration and use of ICT is a remarkable development of the 21st century, probably exceeding in its effects the advent of television in the 1950s. Technological progress is now so rapid that the spread of computers, mobile phones, and the internet is reaching all parts of the globe, although with greatest penetration in the more wealthy countries.

The Kaiser Foundation carried out three similar surveys on media use in 8–18-year-olds in the USA, in 1999, 2004, and 2009. Some changes through the first decade of this century are shown in Table 4. The figures are estimates of the average time spent (in hours:minutes) in a typical day.

Overall, the most time was spent watching television content. This was followed by listening to music, texting on a mobile phone, and

Table 4. Time spent per day on various media activities and with mobile phones by 8-18-year-olds in the USA at three time points

Activity/Time spent (hrs:mins)	1999	2004	2009
Watching television content	3:47	3:51	4:29
Listening to music	1:48	1:44	2:31
Using a computer	0:27	1:02	1:29
Playing video games	0:26	0:49	1:13
Reading print media	0:43	0:43	0:38
Going to films	0:18	0:25	0:25
Total media exposure allowing for multi-tasking	6:19	6:21	7:38
Talking on mobile phone			0:33
Texting on mobile phone			1:35

Source: Kaiser Foundation (2010). *Generation M2: Media in the Lives of 8- to 18-Year-Olds*. 20 January, p. 2. Reproduced with permission from the Kaiser Foundation (www.kff.org).

using a computer. Using a computer increased dramatically over the period, as did playing video games. By 2009 these children and young people used media for over seven and a half hours a day, quite often multi-tasking with two or three media at once (such as downloading music from a computer). This figure does not include the more than two hours a day spent talking, and more frequently texting, on mobile phones. Use of mobile phones was not even asked about in 1999 and not asked about separately from landline phones in 2004.

Ofcom surveys in the UK

In the UK, Ofcom has provided regular surveys of media use in children and young people since 2003, including 12-15-year-olds in their oldest age band. Table 5 shows how access to various media, and ownership of mobile phones, changed from 2007 up

Table 5. Access to and ownership of various media opportunities for 12–15-year-olds in the UK, from Ofcom (2014)

Activity / percentage of young people	2007	2009	2011	2013	2014
Availability in the home					
Internet (PC/laptop/netbook)	77	85	95	94	93
Tablet computer			7	48	71
Games console/player	88	89	93	89	85
Digital video recorder (DVR)	22	43	68	75	76
Radio set	90	90	84	79	75
Smart TV				13	41
Ownership of non-smart and smart phones					
Non-smart phone			46	20	13
Smart phone			41	62	65

Source: Reproduced from Ofcom (2014), *Children and Parents: Media Use and Attitudes Report*, October.

to 2014. Access to the internet increased and reached almost all of this age group by 2011. Noticeable have been dramatic increases in access to DVRs, tablet computers, and smart TVs in the last few years, which have also seen a rapid switch from ownership of non-smart to smart mobile phones. In 2014, ownership of a smart phone was 41 per cent in 12-year-olds rising to 80 per cent in 15-year-olds.

These young people were also asked which of nine media devices they used almost every day. The answers in 2014 in order of popularity were: TV set 80 per cent; mobile phone 69 per cent; PC/laptop 49 per cent; tablet 39 per cent; games console/player 36 per cent; books/magazines/comics 28 per cent; radio 15 per cent; MP3 player 13 per cent; DVD/Blu-ray player 9 per cent. Clearly use of television remains popular, but ICT use (via mobile phones and computers) has rapidly increased; altogether, 12–15-year-olds spent more time on the internet, at 17.2 hours/week, than watching television, at 15.7 hours/week; with gaming taking up 11.2 hours/week.

The Ofcom surveys also asked about what the different media were used for. Mobile phones were used much more for texting than making phone calls (Table 5, cf. also Table 4). In 2014 this was an average of 137 texts per week; 163 for girls compared to 113 for boys. The greater importance of mobile phones for girls was shown when asked which device they would miss the most; 46 per cent of girls said their mobile phone (and 29 per cent of boys); by contrast, 22 per cent of boys said games/console player (and only 3 per cent of girls). Popular activities using mobile phones were arranging to meet friends (71 per cent), messaging friends (53 per cent), looking at photos posted online (47 per cent), and sharing photos they had taken (45 per cent). By contrast, TV was used most for watching full-length films/movies (85 per cent) and a PC/laptop for finding information for school work (73 per cent).

Pew Research Center surveys in the USA

A survey of over 1,000 children and young people aged 8–18 years in the USA was reported by the Pew Research Center on the basis of structured interviews carried out in late 2014 and early 2015. Access to different media devices was 87 per cent for a desktop or laptop computer; 81 per cent for a gaming console; 73 per cent for a smart phone; 58 per cent for a tablet computer; and 15 per cent who had a basic phone (and not a smart phone). (These figures are less than those in Table 5, probably because of the younger ages included.) Findings were similar for boys and girls, except for a gaming console where boys (91 per cent) exceeded girls (70 per cent). This report found that the median number of texts sent per day from mobile phones was thirty. As in the UK, there was a gender difference, the median being forty/day for girls and twenty/day for boys.

Computer games

Computer games have evolved rapidly; they can be used for entertainment and stimulation, for education and training, or for presenting simulations of the real world. They are attractive to young people because they are interactive, players respond to the demands of the game and receive feedback for their performance. The player can develop an identity by interacting with other characters or becoming a character in the game, getting a sense of achievement by progressing to more complex levels and learning more skills. A concern has been that playing computer games can result in social isolation, but some studies have found that adolescent boys especially often play with friends, and that the activity can enhance the amount of time spent with friends. Another concern is that being primarily sedentary (like many media activities), it may be a factor in increasing obesity in young people. Some interactive games, like 'exergames', involve physical activity, but as yet there is little research on their effects on physical health.

Some computer games involve violence. One review summarized findings from 136 studies of violent games. They found that violent game exposure was associated with greater aggressive behaviour, cognition, and affect, and less empathy and prosocial behaviour. This was true of both sexes. However, the effects were relatively small in size. As with the concerns about violence on television, it appears that there can be harmful effects of computer game violence, but that for most young people at least, it is not a major factor in understanding violent behaviour.

The cyberworld in the 21st century

While much use of the internet may be for surfing, emailing, and getting information generally, an increasing use amongst young people has been social networking. Fashions in social networking sites change year-by-year. Bebo and MySpace were popular in the UK in 2009 but their use had fallen dramatically by 2014. The Ofcom 2014 survey found that of 12–15-year-olds going online (around 93 per cent, Table 5), 71 per cent had a social media profile. Most popular by far was Facebook, followed by Instagram, Twitter, Snapchat, and YouTube. The Pew Research Center survey in the USA in 2014–15 also found Facebook to be the most popular (71 per cent), followed by Instagram (52 per cent), Snapchat (41 per cent), Twitter (33 per cent), and Google+ (33 per cent). Mobile phones were widely used to go online. Altogether 24 per cent said that they were online almost constantly; 56 per cent several times a day, 12 per cent once a day, and 6 per cent weekly; only 2 per cent said that they never went online.

Whereas boys seem more interesting in gaming, girls seem more interested in social networking. This is not always evident as regards access. For example, Pew found 70 per cent of girls and 72 per cent of boys had a Facebook account. But it does show up consistently in usage. For example, girls reported an average of 175 Facebook friends compared to 100 for boys. On Instagram, often used for sharing photos and videos, rather more girls used it than boys (61 per cent compared to 44 per cent), but girls especially exceeded boys in the number of followers (a median of 200 compared to 100). On Snapchat, also used for sharing images and videos that are automatically deleted after a period of time, girls' usage again exceeded boys' by 51 per cent to 31 per cent. For Twitter, usage showed a small gender difference (37 per cent girls, 30 per cent boys) but again a large difference in number of followers (girls averaging 116, boys 61). Although it was less frequently used overall, more girls than boys also used Vine (an app that allows users to record and share short video clips), and Tumblr (a microblogging service where users can share mostly visual material).

A European research project, EU Kids Online I (2006–9) and II (2009–11), has examined online activities amongst children and adolescents across a range of EU countries. EU Kids Online I collated available findings on cultural, contextual, and risk issues in children's use of online technologies across twenty-one countries. The internet activities of 9–19-year-olds, in order of frequency, were: searching for information; doing school work; playing games; sending or receiving email; instant messaging; downloading music; doing quizzes; searching shops; visiting sites for hobbies; making a website; visiting sports sites; reading the news; seeking personal information; seeking computer information; visiting chat rooms; posting pictures or stories; and visiting porn sites.

EU Kids Online II examined online activities amongst children and adolescents across twenty-five European countries. A major part of this was a quantitative survey in 2010 of about 1,000 children aged 9–16 years in each country. It encompassed questions about internet use, digital literacy, coping responses, perceptions, and safety practices. The survey found that 93 per cent of 9–16-year-olds went online at least weekly, and 60 per cent daily; for 15–16-year-olds, 80 per cent went on the internet daily. The main activities online for the 13–16-year-olds were school work (89 per cent over the past month), watching video clips

(86 per cent), visiting a social networking profile (81 per cent), playing games (80 per cent), instant messaging (77 per cent), and sending/receiving emails (75 per cent). A majority—73 per cent of 13–14-year-olds and 82 per cent of 15–16-year-olds—had a social networking profile.

Opportunities on the internet

Social networking site profiles are now an important aspect of affirming identity, certainly for most adolescents in Western societies. Just as teenagers decorate their bedrooms with images and posters, they also design and adorn their personal web pages and their profiles. Many are on a number of different social networking sites, and these can provide different social contexts for different aspects of their identity.

Adolescents move flexibly between many forms of media use and communication, facilitated by smart phones that can access the internet. Often, they are sustaining friendships that are also present in the offline world. However, the internet helps maintain a very wide circle of friends. One study in Israel of 11–18-year-olds showed that Instant Messaging (IMing) with friends online provided emotional relief for adolescents who were feeling distressed. They could share worries with those they chose to communicate with, in an intimate and private space. A survey carried out in the UK for Safer Internet Day in 2015 found that 63 per cent of 11–16-year-olds said that they were closer to their friends because of the internet. As one girl is quoted as saying, 'I like to share my art, my edits and make quizzes and stories and share them on websites like Tumblr, Instagram, Wattpad and Quotev'.

Risks on the internet

The majority of online activity is sociable and useful or enjoyable, but there are risks as well as opportunities. Risks have been categorized into four main areas: aggressive (threats, cyberbullying), sexual (sexting, pornography, grooming), value-related (e.g. visiting extremist sites, pro-anorexia, or suicide sites), or commercial (such as pop-up advertisements). They can also be divided into content risks (the young person receives unwanted content), contact risks (often with an adult-initiated online interaction which requires the young person to participate), and conduct risks (where the young person is part of a wider peer-to-peer or networked interaction).

A focus of the EU Kids Online survey was on risks and safety on the internet. Giving out personal information too readily or inappropriately was the most common risky behaviour. Other common online risks were sexting (sending or forwarding sexually explicit messages, images, or photos to others), exposure to inappropriate content (such as pornographic materials, or content of a violent or racist nature), and receiving unwelcome contact, perhaps sexual (e.g. grooming, sexual harassment) or being cyberbullied. Meeting an online contact offline without adequate precautions, which can be particularly dangerous, was much less frequent.

There were gender differences in risk, with boys more likely to be involved in conduct risks, and girls more affected by content and contact risks. Exposure to risks increased with age: 49 per cent of 13–14-year-olds and 63 per cent of 15–16-year-olds said they had encountered one or more risks. However, not all risks were perceived by adolescents as harmful; for example, sexting was only perceived as harmful in certain circumstances. A minority, 12 per cent of 13–14-year-olds and 15 per cent of 15–16-year-olds, said that they had been bothered or upset by something on the internet.

According to the UK Safer Internet survey in 2015, 65 per cent of 13–14-year-olds and 70 per cent of 15–16-year-olds felt able to cope with negative online experiences. Besides basic e-safety procedures such as privacy settings and blocking someone who is being mean or threatening, support from peers and parents can be important. Parents are best being involved in and discussing an adolescent's use of the internet and SNS, but not being too intrusive or over-regulatory so that the young person's autonomy is also respected (Chapter 4).

Internet addiction

There have been concerns about the effects of spending so much time on ICT activities. The EU Kids Online project found that about 29 per cent of 13–14-year-olds and 36 per cent of 15–16-year-olds said that they had spent less time than they should with friends, family, or doing schoolwork because of time spent online. Excessive internet use, often referred to as internet addiction or problematic internet use, increases the chances of experiencing risks online as well as taking time away from offline activities.

The Kaiser Foundation report found an association of greater internet use with lower grades at school. About half (47 per cent) of heavy media users reported getting low grades, compared to about a quarter (23 per cent) of light media users. According to a study in Finland with 10- and 13-year-olds, parents were happy with their children using the internet for learning and information seeking, but relations were less good if they did a lot digital game playing, internet surfing, and email chatting. Findings were more complicated as regards peer relationships. A lot of digital game playing did relate negatively to quality of friendships, but a lot of emailing and internet chatting went with feeling less lonely with peers.

A moral panic?

Newspaper headlines such as 'Too much internet use can damage teenagers' brains' (*Daily Mail*, 15 July 2011) and 'Are social networking sites really infantilising our teenagers?' (*Guardian*, 22 February 2009) reflect what may be genuine concerns about excessive internet use, but may also be seen as reflecting a moral panic, in which worries about poorly understood phenomena are built up by the media into something more sensational. In her book *It's Complicated*, published in 2014, danah boyd acknowledged the risks and possible harm of internet use, but argued that generally the concerns of parents and others are misplaced, and that in most cases any addiction of teenagers is to social networking rather than to the technology itself.

In discussing teenagers' use of social networking sites, boyd used the phrase *networked publics* to describe how adolescents can congregate on virtual communities online, just as they might previously have congregated in public spaces such as shopping malls. This is now where they hang out with their friends. She also argued that these networked publics create new opportunities or affordances: persistence (the durability of online expressions and content); visibility (the potential audience); spreadability (the ease with which content can be shared); and searchability (the ability to find content). In the US context at least, she argued that there are reduced offline opportunities, with parents increasingly concerned about safety; and that 'social media…is a release valve, allowing youth to reclaim meaningful sociality as a tool for managing the pressures and limitations around them'.

Chapter 6
Risk-taking, antisocial behaviour, and delinquency

Risk is defined in the *Encarta World English Dictionary* as the danger that injury, damage, or loss will occur. Risky behaviours are common in adolescence. Common categories of risk are aggressive and violent behaviours, reckless driving, casual and unsafe sex, drug use, and risky online behaviours. The costs of such behaviours may be incurred by the individual him- or herself, and/or it may be incurred by others. A similar category is reckless behaviour, meaning behaviour carried out without apparent concern for the consequences.

Antisocial behaviour can be defined as being annoying, inconsiderate, or indifferent to the comfort or needs of neighbours, or to society as a whole (*Encarta*). Common examples are graffiti, vandalism, petty theft, and joyriding. Here the harm is to others, although some antisocial behaviour is risky in terms of the antisocial person possibly incurring sanctions. This will especially be the case with delinquent behaviour, defined as antisocial or illegal behaviour or acts, especially by young people (*Encarta*). Many researchers use a narrower definition of delinquency as illegal or criminal behaviour, such as stealing, assault, illegal drug use, or under-age sex. However, others prefer the broader definition of delinquency as antisocial or problem behaviour.

Incidence and age changes

Some categories of antisocial or risk-taking behaviour are quite common in adolescence. Table 6 shows some data gathered in 2003 in the Crime and Justice Survey, a nationally representative survey of young people carried out for the Home Office in England and Wales. The figures show the percentage who reported being involved, at least once in each category, over the last twelve months. For most categories (although not all) there is a peak in incidence in the 14–16-year-old age range. Indeed, 41 per cent at this age range admit to being involved in at least one of these antisocial acts over the last year. Thus, at least some limited or minor involvement in antisocial behaviour can be seen as a common if not normative feature of adolescence.

However, different kinds of antisocial behaviour show different trajectories. Another example of this is shown in Table 7, which narrows down onto the 14–16-year-old age range. This was a longitudinal study based on a representative survey for the former Department of Children, Schools and Families (DCSF), in England, using data from 2004 to 2006. The researchers examined risky behaviour which they categorized as externalizing (four categories of antisocial behaviour which harm other people or property), and three categories of internalizing risky behaviours (which may harm the young people themselves).

It is apparent that the four externalizing categories show a decline from 14 to 16 years. Putting this together with Table 6, which includes younger ages, it appears that around 14 years is a peak for many of what might be considered to be the more minor types of antisocial behaviour. However, smoking and drinking show a considerable increase from 14 to 16—perhaps as cigarettes and alcoholic drinks become easier to obtain at older ages. Of course, a few years later many adults smoke and drink alcohol perfectly legally, and these might only be

Table 6. Incidence (percentages) of six types of antisocial behaviour, by age, in England and Wales, over a one-year period

Category/ Age	10–11	12–13	14–16	17–19	20–25	Male	Female
Public disturbance	9	18	26	18	9	19	12
Neighbour complaint	13	11	13	14	13	16	10
Carrying weapons	3	5	9	9	4	10	2
Graffiti	2	5	10	4	1	4	3
Racial harassment	1	1	3	3	1	2	1
Joyriding	0	0.5	3	3	1	2	1
Any of the above	22	29	41	35	22	35	23

Source: England and Wales data, adapted from Home Office 2003 survey, Ruth Hayward and Clare Sharp, Home Office Findings 245, 2005. Crown copyright information is reproduced with the permission of the Controller of HMSO and the Queen's Printer for Scotland.

Table 7. Incidence (percentages) of seven types of risky behaviour, by age, in England, over a one-year period

Category/Age	14	15	16
Externalizing			
Taking part in fighting or a public disturbance	19	18	16
Shoplifting	12	8	7
Vandalism of a public property	11	9	8
Graffitiing	7	6	6
Internalizing			
Drinking a proper alcoholic drink (more often than once a month)	17	29	39
Smoking cigarettes (at least sometimes)	8	16	22
Playing truant (more than just the odd day or lesson)	5	8	9

Source: Adapted from Andreas Cebulla and Wojtek Tomaszewski (2009). *Risky Behavior and Social Activities, Research Report to Department for Children, Schools and Families.* London: DCSF, Figure 2.1.

considered risky behaviour in certain circumstances (e.g. pregnancy) or if carried to excess.

Some data from the USA is shown in Table 8. This is from the Youth Risk Behavior Surveillance (YRBS) survey, carried out annually for the Department of Health and Human Services. The 2013 survey was given to 13,633 young people in grades 9–12 (so about 14–18 years) across most states. The survey does not give data for younger ages, but from 14 years on, fighting declines. Carrying a weapon or gun does not show much age change, although the levels are frighteningly high. Carrying weapons (such as a knife) is about twice as frequent in the USA as in England and Wales (compare Table 6). Again, smoking cigarettes, drinking, and marijuana use increase with age.

Table 8. Incidence (percentages) of being in a physical fight or injured in a physical fight, carrying a weapon or gun, and three types of drug use, by grade and gender, in the USA, over a one-year period

Category/ Grade (age)	9 (14–15)	10 (15–16)	11 (16–17)	12 (17–18)	Male	Female
Fighting						
In a physical fight over last 12 months	28	26	24	19	30	19
Injured in a physical fight over last 12 months	3	3	3	3	4	2
Weapons						
Carried a weapon in last 30 days	18	18	18	18	28	8
Carried a gun in last 30 days	6	5	6	6	9	2
Drug use						
Smoking cigarettes at least once in last 30 days	10	13	21	19	16	15
Drinking alcohol at least once in last 30 days	24	31	39	47	34	36
Using marijuana at least once in last 30 days	18	24	26	28	25	22

Source: USA data, adapted from YRBS 2013 survey.

Using self-reporting surveys is one way of examining incidence and age changes. Anonymity is guaranteed in such surveys, but they do rely on respondents being reasonably truthful and accurate in admitting to what may often be sanctioned and sometimes illegal behaviours. A different approach is to look at statistics of actual behaviours. This is readily done for delinquency, taken as criminal acts and recorded as such. Statistics on delinquency very consistently show a sharp rise at adolescence, which peaks and then is followed by a slower decline. One influential study on delinquency has been the Cambridge Study in Delinquent Development. This was an in-depth longitudinal study of 411 working class boys, born in London around 1953, which was followed up through adolescence and into adulthood. The peak age for first arrests was 14–15 years. The incidence of more serious criminal activities usually peaked in later adolescence or their early 20s, before declining steadily through adult life. Again, trajectories vary for different kinds of criminal behaviour, but adolescence clearly emerges as a period when many kinds of delinquent antisocial behaviours are most common.

Another quite different approach, used to look at changes in risky behaviour with age, has been to use experimental tasks. For example in gambling tasks, you might opt for a bet with a good chance of winning a small prize or one with a small chance of winning a large prize. The latter is risky, as you will most likely lose the money placed on the bet, but some people will be tempted to go for this.

In one study, these kinds of gambling tasks were given to four age groups: pre-teens (9–11 years), early adolescents (12–15 years), later adolescents (16–18 years), and adults (20–35 years). All participants were males. The proportion of risky choices increased significantly from pre-teens to early adolescence, where it was highest. It fell off somewhat by later adolescence, and adults were the least risk-taking. The investigators also got ratings of emotional involvement, such as relief at winning or regret at losing, and these too were highest in the early adolescents. The early adolescent peak in risk-taking has been found in a number of studies, but it does seem to be most marked when emotions are involved or when peers are present. Another study, with 11–16-year-old adolescent females, did not find an age change in risk-taking when their emotions were not so involved.

Gender differences

Generally, males are more involved in risky and antisocial behaviours than females. For example in the Home Office survey (Table 6), over the whole age range, 35 per cent of males but only 23 per cent of females were involved in at least one category of antisocial behaviour; and males scored higher on all six categories. The DCSF survey (Table 7) found males significantly higher than females for the externalizing antisocial behaviours, but not for the internalizing ones. The YRBS survey (Table 8) shows males greatly exceeding females in the fighting and weapons categories, but shows little difference in the drug taking categories. A meta-analysis of 150 studies on risk-taking, which reported gender differences, showed that in most categories and at most ages, males scored higher. However, females scored somewhat higher on smoking in the adolescent period, and there was not much gender difference in drinking or other kinds of drug taking.

Historical changes

The YRBS surveys in the USA have been carried out annually since 1991, and they give a detailed picture of changes since then. The picture is generally positive so far as many risk-taking behaviours are concerned. Rates of physical fighting and carrying weapons have declined—although the rate of weapon carrying did level off in recent years. Rates of cigarette, alcohol, and marijuana use have also declined throughout most of this period.

Factors affecting risk-taking, antisocial behaviour, and delinquency

Although minor or occasional antisocial acts may be frequent in adolescence, not all adolescents get involved, and many do not get involved a lot. Only a relatively small proportion of young people get heavily involved. For example in the Home Office survey (Table 6), of those who admitted to any antisocial behaviour, about two-thirds had only been involved in one category, and about one-fifth in two. Only a small proportion, about 12 per cent in the teenage years, had been involved in three or more categories.

Apart from age and gender, many studies have looked at what risk factors may be involved in explaining why some young people get more involved than others. For example, the Cambridge study of boys in London reported on risk factors for delinquency. The seven most powerful predictors from middle childhood of chronic delinquency in adolescence were: troublesomeness in school; hyperactivity/poor concentration; low intelligence and poor attainment; family criminality; family poverty; and poor parental child rearing. If the family moved out of London, however, this move was found to be a protective factor!

The Home Office study also reported on risk factors for the kinds of antisocial behaviours shown in Table 6. Besides age and gender, these included personality factors such as risk-taking and disregard for others; a poor relationship with parents; a poor school environment; association with delinquent peer groups; drug use and alcohol consumption; and living in a disordered neighbourhood. The DCSF study (Table 7) identified poor relations with parents, living in a single-parent family, having negative attitudes to school, associating with peers with similar attitudes, and experiencing bullying as being risk factors for both externalizing and internalizing risky behaviours. This study also identified some protective factors associated with a lower likelihood of risky behaviours which they called *self-development activities*. These included playing a musical instrument, doing community work, attending religious classes, and reading for pleasure.

There is a lot of consistency in these different reports. *Social control theory*, developed by Travis Hirschi, argues that antisocial behaviour is less likely when the young person has a stake in social institutions such as the family, school, or clubs and societies. Some bonding or commitment to these groups acts as a control on temptations to carry out risky or delinquent behaviours.

In particular, parenting and family factors have been implicated in many studies of delinquency. For example, a longitudinal study of more than 400 French-Canadian boys in Montreal examined the impact of family transition on the development of delinquency between 12 and 15 years. They looked especially at the effects of divorce and remarriage, comparing cases where this happened while the boy was 6–11 years old and those where he was 12–15 years. They did not find divorce to have a main effect on delinquency. However, they did find that boys in families experiencing a remarriage while they were aged 12–15 were more likely to become delinquent. These boys saw their parents as less expressive and less likely to monitor their behaviour. Besides lack of parental supervision, other predictors of delinquency were poverty and academic failure.

Parental supervision and monitoring of behaviour seems important, but it needs to be done sensitively (Chapter 4). Two theoretical perspectives suggest that certain kinds of parental behaviour might exacerbate antisocial behaviours. *Psychological reactance theory* argues that dogmatic prohibitions and restrictive rules about behaviour can lead to anger and rejection of authority, producing a kind of boomerang effect. Rather similarly, *self-determination theory* argues that autonomy is strongly valued and that, if this is frustrated, it can lead to anger and oppositional defiance. One series of studies in the Netherlands found good evidence that very controlling and unresponsive parenting did indeed predict behaviours such as rule-breaking, fighting, and stealing in adolescence.

However, another common risk factor is association with delinquent peers. In secondary schools the values of some antisocial peer groups can be very different from those of teachers, with a rejection of academic success and a noticeable level of truanting (Table 7). Given that we tend to choose friends who are similar to ourselves, it is not obvious that peers actually cause delinquent behaviour, but there is evidence that this is often the case. Early maturing girls may be drawn into delinquent behaviour through choosing to associate with older peers who are more likely to engage in antisocial acts (Chapter 2).

One longitudinal study of 1,354 juvenile offenders in the USA aimed to disentangle the effects of selection (choosing antisocial peers to affiliate with), and socialization (the effects of delinquent peers on the individual). In middle adolescence there was evidence that both processes were at work. The effect of delinquent peers was strong in later adolescence, but declined after age 20 as young people developed greater autonomy. Another longitudinal study, of boys aged 14–16 years in Montreal, Canada, reached similar conclusions as regards delinquency and drug use in youth gangs. Delinquent behaviour was much higher in gang members, as might be expected. This appeared to be due to both selection (delinquent youth chooses to join a gang) and facilitation (youth becomes delinquent through the influence of other gang members).

One factor which may be at work in understanding the effects of antisocial or delinquent peers is status and *reputation enhancement theory*. Status in the peer group is very important to adolescents (Chapter 4). Reputation enhancement theory argues that engaging in activities consonant with the attitudes and values of your peer group is likely to enhance your status in that group. For non-delinquent groups, antisocial behaviour might be seen as trouble-making and a reason for rejection or exclusion. However, a delinquent group will have quite different values. To enhance your status in such a group, it may be beneficial to not only join in antisocial activities, but to initiate them and show that you are more daring than the others. In short, antisocial behaviour might be a reason for exclusion in some peer groups, but a reason for inclusion in others.

Internet risks—parents and peers

The internet has enabled a new zone of experience in which further kinds of risky behaviour can be engaged in (Chapter 5). However, similar factors around parents and peers appear to operate in this domain as well. A study in Singapore with 13–14-year-olds examined contact risks and privacy risks on social networking sites. Contact risks were assessed in terms of adding people they had never met to their friend lists. Privacy risks were assessed in terms of amounts of personal information on the site and the privacy settings used. Attempts by parents to use restrictive control methods were counter-productive in reducing risks, whereas discussion-based tactics helped reduce contact risks. However, discussion with peers seemed to increase privacy risks. Another study in Singapore was of juvenile delinquents in the 13–18-year age range who were in counselling or rehabilitation. Most used Facebook as a site to chat, and post and comment on status updates. They enjoyed giving and receiving peer affirmation on this site. Many of these adolescents were trying to put their delinquency behind them. But an unfortunate aspect of their Facebook use, which came out in interviews, was that this additional online audience could make the process more difficult. There were pressures to display group loyalty and endorse delinquent acts. Nevertheless, some used Facebook to signal a change:

> Yeah, through my post... like I say, 'I'm sick and tired of this life. I just want to change'.

Adolescence-limited and life-course offenders

Terrie Moffitt has made a distinction between *adolescence-limited* and *life-course persistent* offending. A similar distinction is sometimes referred to as *early starters* and *late starters* for delinquency. In adolescence-limited offending, children follow a fairly normal developmental path, but show some antisocial and delinquent behaviours during adolescence, as they enter puberty and the maturity gap (Chapter 2), and get drawn into the risk-taking behaviours of antisocial peer groups. Some delinquent behaviours demonstrate autonomy and give status with peers. However, offences tend to be minor and to fall off as adulthood approaches. In life-course persistent offending, children are aggressive and disruptive in primary and middle school, and often peer rejected at that time. However, in secondary school they associate with others like themselves and form the core of antisocial peer groups. They commit offences from a relatively early age and are more likely to re-offend. They are less influenced by peer pressures, but may act as role magnets, attracting adolescence-limited peers as co-offenders.

This typology is consistent with many findings, including the somewhat normative nature of minor delinquent acts in adolescence, but that only a much smaller minority engage persistently in many different types. The Cambridge study of 411 boys in London supported this kind of distinction. Of those convicted of an offence early, between 10 and 15 years, twenty-three boys (about one-third of all offenders) were chronic offenders, having at least six offences by 18 years. These boys were responsible for half of all the convictions from the 411 boys in total. By contrast, none of those first convicted after 15 classified as chronic offenders.

Risk-taking, puberty, and brain changes

The relatively new neuroscience perspective (Chapter 1) sees increased risk-taking as related to brain changes in adolescence.

There is an increased sensitivity to rejection by peers (Chapter 4), and also a temporary change in the balance of sensation-seeking as opposed to behavioural control (Figure 4). In one study in the USA with about 1,000 participants aged 10 to 30 years, sensation-seeking was linked to pubertal maturation. It increased from 10 to 15 years before declining. In contrast, behavioural control was unrelated to puberty and increased steadily from 10 years onwards.

Furthermore, the presence of peers can enhance risky behaviour, especially in adolescence. Another study in the USA used three age groups: adolescents (14–18), young adults (19–22) and adults (24–9). They were given a simulated driving task with traffic intersections. Sometimes they were alone, sometimes they were told that peers were watching through a monitor. The researchers measured risky decisions in this task. When alone, there was not much difference in risk-taking, but when told peers were watching, only the adolescents showed increased risk-taking. In addition the researchers assessed brain activity using fMRI scans. In the peer watching condition, the adolescents showed more brain activity in the reward sensitivity areas of the brain, but no change in the behavioural control areas. In real-life situations, the reward could be showing off to gain status with peers.

This perspective suggests that risky behaviours can be understood in terms of the balance of emotional impulse and cognitive control, plus other factors such as enhanced peer influence. It does not mean that adolescents are deficient in their cognitive understanding of the risks involved.

Two models compared

Focusing especially on risky behaviour in adolescents, Bruce Ellis and colleagues in 2012 compared two models of explanation. These were the *developmental psychopathology model* and the *evolutionary model*. Both models acknowledge the influence of poor parenting, disaffiliation from school, association with like-minded peers, and deprived environments. But the developmental psychopathology model also sees risk-taking as maladaptive behaviour, a sign that something has gone wrong in development. This is because of the costs of risky behaviour to oneself and others.

However, an exclusive emphasis on costs ignores the balance of possible benefits. All of us take some risks, and we balance out short-term and long-term benefits against costs. This of course is consistent with social control theory. If you have strong family or school bonds, the short-term benefit of stealing from a store will be outweighed by the longer-term cost of disapproval from parents and possible expulsion from school. However, if you do not have such strong bonds, the cost–benefit balance may shift.

Ellis and colleagues proposed the evolutionary model, taking insights from evolutionary theory (Chapter 1). They suggested that such a perspective provides five key insights. First, adolescence is a time of establishing status in the peer group and, ultimately, reproductive success. Competitive tendencies increase. Risky behaviours such as sexual promiscuity can be advantageous in terms of learning about your mate preferences and desirability. Second, risky and aggressive behaviours such as bullying may help get resources and enhance status. Third, the cost–benefit ratio of risky behaviours will vary depending on the prevailing environment. In unpredictable and stressful environments, a definite short-term benefit may be valued more highly than any long-term cost that might never be incurred. Fourth, sexual selection theory predicts that males have more to gain and less to lose from risky behaviours. Fifth, compared to the environment of evolutionary adaptedness (Chapter 1), contemporary adolescents are in large, same-age peer groups that may increase risky behaviours. Smaller, mixed-age peer groups may provide a more natural context and one that increases prosocial behaviours.

Not all these insights are new. Certainly reputation enhancement theory did not see risky behaviour as maladaptive. The evolutionary model is consistent with the neuroscience perspective, but focuses on functions rather than mechanisms (on 'why' rather than 'how'). It does provide an overall explanatory framework and, like other theories, it does have implications for intervention.

Interventions

Even if sometimes adaptive for the individual, adolescent risk-taking and delinquency, especially when more than occasional or minor acts, has significant costs for society. Car crashes, unwanted pregnancies, juvenile crimes such as thefts and assaults need to be reduced as much as is feasible. From the social control theory viewpoint, improving parenting skills and parent–adolescent relationships, providing an encouraging and well-organized school environment, and involvement in productive self-development activities would be important steps.

What may not be so useful are social skills training or empathy training programmes, which may be off-target. These kinds of peer-based interventions can have what are called iatrogenic, or negative, effects. If antisocial children are selected to participate in a group-based intervention of this kind, then they may actually share and reinforce each other's values. As reputation enhancement theory would suggest, they may choose to enhance their status in this new group by engaging in antisocial behaviours. This could outweigh any possible benefits of the training programme itself.

The neuroscience perspective suggests that adolescents are aware of risks but are impulsive, so strategies to make risk-taking behaviours more difficult would be recommended. Examples might be regulating alcohol sales, raising the legal driving age, and improving access to contraceptives. The evolutionary model too argues that exhortations and programmes to raise awareness of risks may be counter-productive, as they could increase the status of the risk-taking activities. Besides tackling the adverse environmental conditions that make risk-taking more likely, it points to the need to provide alternative routes for adolescents to maintain reputation with their peer group. These should still be status-enhancing, but not so risky for them or potentially harmful to others; sports participation might be one such example.

Chapter 7
Internalizing disorders and adolescent mental health

Internalizing disorders refer to problematic or harmful behaviours directed at oneself rather than at others. Although illegal drug use (Chapter 6) can be considered as an internalizing behaviour, the term 'internalizing disorder' is primarily used to refer to sadness, mood disruption, withdrawal, and depression. More serious indicators are thoughts about suicide and actual attempts at suicide. Eating disorders, including anorexia and bulimia, are another category of internalizing behaviour. Eating disorders overlap to some extent with obesity, also considered in this chapter.

Mood disruption and emotional turmoil

Mood disruption can be defined as feeling depressed or having fluctuating moods. There is a long history of seeing adolescence as a time of moodiness and emotional turmoil, with both Hall as a psychologist and Freud as a psychoanalyst stressing this in the early years of the 20th century (Chapter 1). These views held sway for some time. In 1962 Peter Blos developed the psychoanalytic approach further in his book *On Adolescence*. Here, he called adolescence a second individuation process. The first individuation process was the transition an infant makes to becoming a more self-reliant toddler, which is often accompanied by tantrums. Blos regarded adolescence as a parallel process of transition to independence, at a later stage. It too was naturally accompanied by ambivalence and regression. Indeed, the concept of adolescence as a turbulent, rebellious period remained popular in the 1960s and 1970s, as noted in Erikson's work on identity crisis at that time (Chapter 3). But in the later decades of the 20th century there was some reaction against this, with some researchers arguing that such difficulties in adolescence were not characteristic of all adolescents, and were often of a rather minor nature. John Coleman proposed a focal theory of adolescence, whereby developmental tasks or difficulties did not all come at once, but were spread through the adolescent years. This implied that they could be managed one by one, rather than bringing about some kind of crisis.

The Isle of Wight study

An attempt to settle the issue about emotional turmoil was made by Michael Rutter and colleagues in an article entitled *Adolescent turmoil: fact or fiction?*. They reported findings from a comprehensive study of all the 14–15-year-olds on the Isle of Wight, off the south coast of England. Altogether there were 2,303 young people in this age range. A random sample of 200 were given detailed assessments and had an interview with a psychiatrist. From this it emerged that on the survey questionnaire, between one-fifth and one-quarter (21 per cent males, 23 per cent females) said that they often felt miserable or depressed. Rather more (42 per cent males, 48 per cent females) reported having miserable feelings according to the psychiatrists, although less than a third of these actually looked sad in the interview. About one in seven (13 per cent) were actually diagnosed as having some psychiatric disorder.

Is this a case of a glass being one-sevenths full, or six-sevenths empty? Here it is important to see how these figures compare with younger or older ages. Fortunately the researchers could compare figures for psychiatric disorder at 14–15 with those for the same children at age 10, as there had been a previous survey some years earlier. They also got assessments for the parents of the 14–15-year-olds as an adult sample. The findings, based on parental interview data for all three ages, suggested that the incidence of any psychiatric disorder was around 12 per cent at 10 years, 13 per cent at 14–15 years, and 10 per cent in adults. There was a modest peak in adolescence, but the differences were small and most adolescents were not seriously disturbed. It was concluded in the report that 'adolescent turmoil is a fact, not a fiction, but its psychiatric importance has probably been over-estimated in the past'. This conclusion is, of course, limited historically, the study being about forty years old at the time of writing. Also the Isle of Wight was convenient in terms of getting a complete local sample, but consisting of small villages and towns, it is a very different environment from modern urban life in the UK.

Mood disruption and feelings of sadness

To assess mood more directly, an ingenious study in the USA, carried out in the 1990s, asked 10–14-year-olds to wear an electronic pager for a week. In response to randomized signals, they recorded how they felt emotionally. The 12–14-year-olds experienced significantly more negative emotional affect than the 10–11-year-olds. The researchers also gave these young people a life-events questionnaire, asking about significant things affecting them recently. Greater negative affect was related to negative life events. These life events were generally around family, school, and peers.

This study provides another source of evidence that internalizing issues such as sadness increase from around 10 to 14 years. But how about after 14 years? Table 9 gives some data from the Youth Risk Behavior Surveillance (YRBS) survey 2013 in the USA, covering approximately 14–18 years. It can be seen that around 30 per cent of young people reported feeling sad or hopeless

Table 9. Incidence (percentages) of four measures of depression or suicidal attempts, by grade and gender, in the USA, over a one-year period

Category / grade (age)	9 (14–15)	10 (15–16)	11 (16–17)	12 (17–18)	Male	Female
Felt sad or hopeless during the last 12 months	29	29	32	29	21	39
Seriously considered attempting suicide during the last 12 months	17	17	18	15	12	22
Attempted suicide during the last 12 months	9	9	8	6	5	11
Suicide attempt treated by doctor or nurse during the last 12 months	3	3	3	2	2	4

Source: USA data adapted from the YRBS 2013 survey.

during the last twelve months. This was defined in the survey as feeling like this almost every day for two or more weeks in a row so that they stopped doing some usual activities. There is not really much change in this between 14 and 17 years.

Depression

Sadness and depression can be seen as on a continuum. *Depressed mood* is something everyone is likely to experience at some point in life, but often transiently. In this sense it is a normal response to an adverse life event or stress. A *depressive syndrome* is when this is more enduring, and accompanied by anxiety, low self-esteem, guilt feelings, and maybe other problems such as loneliness or sleep disturbance. Although not precise, the YRBS data on sadness may be picking up this kind of degree of depression. A major *depressive disorder* is diagnosed when there is profound unhappiness, hopelessness, and other symptoms such as abnormal guilt feelings, reduced concentration, eating disorder, and suicidal thoughts or self-harm.

Some insight into issues affecting adolescents with depression comes from a study in Finland. The researchers worked with seventy adolescents aged 15–17 years, who had been referred for psychiatric outpatient treatment, usually for depression. The adolescents provided data over the internet, writing a short essay on their current concerns and life situation. Analysis of these essays revealed four main themes. The first was *relationships*. Here, the main concerns were friends, family, and dating. For example one adolescent wrote, 'I want to develop my social skills', indicating a lack of confidence in this area. Some were concerned about exclusion from friendship groups, some about conflicts with parents, some with being let down by dating partners. The second theme was *daily actions*. Here two main concerns were school and ability to function. For example, one adolescent wrote, 'it is extremely difficult to begin to do something'. Some found it difficult to cope with school pressures. Others could not do things they would normally enjoy, like going to the gym. The third theme was *identity*. Issues here were poor self-esteem and anxieties about the future. One adolescent wrote, 'I have extremely poor self-confidence'. There were often anxieties about their physical appearance and weight. Other concerns were about the challenges of independence and how they were going to cope in the future. The fourth theme was *well-being*. The two main concerns here were ways of thinking and mental health in general. One adolescent wrote, 'I would like to manage my feelings better and even accept the worse periods, too'. For some their lives seemed messed up and they could not think clearly about things. Others had concerns about coping with feelings of anger, sadness, and mood swings. These researchers also used the internet platform on which the data was gathered to offer support via exercises and weekly feedback around reflection and self-help.

Suicidal thoughts and suicide attempts

A very serious outcome of depression, often compounded by other factors, can be thoughts about suicide (suicidal ideation), self-harming, attempts at suicide, and in some tragic cases, actual suicide. As one of the adolescents in the Finnish study (discussed earlier) wrote, 'I find dark elements in my life: sad, anger (lots lots lots of anger), desperation and pain. I feel like this life is just a race with death and I'm just waiting for the helping hand …'.

While completed suicides are thankfully rare, much larger numbers of younger people sometimes think of suicide or they self-harm in some way. Table 9 shows such data from the YRBS 2013 survey in the USA. With about 17 per cent of young people seriously considering attempting suicide in the last twelve months and 8 per cent saying they have actually attempted it, these figures appear alarmingly high. The figures do show some modest age decrease by 17–18 years.

Self-report surveys have limitations, and one might wonder how accurate these figures are. But a study of young people aged 10–17 years in sixteen states of the USA found that suicide was the third leading cause of death, after unintentional injury and homicide. Evidence from legal and medical reports suggested that the main causes of suicides were general relationship problems with friends or parents (51 per cent); intimate relationship problems with a boy/girl friend or parents in the case of teen pregnancy (27 per cent); and school problems (26 per cent). In nearly half of cases (42 per cent), some recent or impending life stress or crisis was present.

Gender differences

It is noticeable from Table 9 that on all the measures, females are scoring about twice as high as males. This gender imbalance is quite characteristic of many internalizing disorders in adolescence, including eating disorders (discussed later in this chapter). It is the opposite of many externalizing problems (Chapter 6), while for drug-taking there is not much gender difference. These differences between male and female adolescents may be related to different coping strategies, rather than to different causes of stress. For example, the study of suicides in the USA, discussed earlier, found that the circumstances leading to suicide did not vary greatly by gender. However, in response to stress, males appear more prone to act out in risky or aggressive behaviours, whereas females seem more prone to depression and self-harm.

Risk factors

Besides being female, many other risk factors for depressive disorders in adolescence have been identified. There is often a family history of depression, which might be related to genetic factors. However, some links are also found in adoptive families, pointing to the importance of parenting styles. Severe physical punishment by parents, affectionless control, rejection, and abuse strongly predict adolescent depression.

A study in the USA looked at risk factors for suicide attempts in 9th and 11th grade students (about 14–15 and 16–17 years). Depression was a risk factor at both ages. At 9th grade other risk factors included use of illegal drugs and homosexual orientation. At 11th grade, risk factors included sexual abuse, being in counselling, and being of 'other' race or ethnicity (mainly Asian or Native American).

Homosexual orientation might be a risk factor because of homophobic bullying. It is well established that lesbian, gay, or bisexual (LGB) young people are more at risk of being bullied. A study of over 4,000 pupils in English schools followed them from ages 13–14 for six years until they had left school. Those who identified themselves as LGB (4.5 per cent of the total sample) experienced a lot more victimization than did heterosexual pupils. LGB pupils were also more unhappy or depressed, and the researchers estimated that about one-half of the increased depression could be attributed to the experiences of being bullied.

Of course, being bullied also affects pupils who are not LGB. Lack of self-esteem and depression are known to be likely outcomes of prolonged victimization experiences. For example, a study of Austrian pupils aged 14–19 years assessed depression and psychosomatic symptoms, such as having stomach aches, in relation to being bullied. The non-involved children scored lowest for both these measures. Those who had experienced either traditional/offline bullying or cyber bullying scored higher; and those who had experienced both traditional and cyber bullying scored particularly highly.

Protective factors, resilience, and interventions

Stresses such as relationship problems, school difficulties, and concerns about appearance may impact on many adolescents, but some clearly cope better than others. Protective factors have been identified in contrast to risk factors. These include academic achievement, involvement in extracurricular activities, and positive relationships with adults outside the family.

Resilience can be defined as doing well in spite of adversity. Doing well can mean using successful coping strategies. These will depend on the situation, but typically include seeking social support or counselling, and engaging in constructive problem-solving. In the study in the USA (mentioned earlier), a protective factor was using systematic problem-solving skills in thinking about their problems. Less successful strategies are to try and ignore the difficulties; to engage in further internalizing behaviours such as self-harm or illegal drug use; or to engage in externalizing behaviours such as fighting and dangerous risk-taking.

Interventions can build on our knowledge of risk and protective factors. Counselling can be provided both face-to-face or via the internet. Some intervention programmes encourage problem-solving skills. For example a six-step model is: 1. Stop, calm down, and think before you act. 2. Articulate the problem and how you feel. 3. Set a positive goal. 4. Think of many solutions. 5. Think ahead to the consequences. 6. Try the best plan. Other programmes may focus on more specific issues or stresses. These might, for example, be how to cope with parental death or divorce; or how to avoid excessive drug use.

Obesity

Obesity is generally assessed in terms of body mass index (BMI). This is defined as the body weight divided by the square of the body height. It can be used to categorize people as underweight, normal weight, overweight, or obese. Obesity is traditionally seen as an energy balance disorder, and is influenced by nutritionally poor diet and low physical activity. However, there are also psychosocial components of obesity, notably how the person sees and copes with weight issues, and the family and society context. Thus, some researchers now argue for a more shared approach to dealing with obesity and eating disorders (next section).

Obesity, often starting in childhood and adolescence, has become an issue of major concern in many Western countries. A study of 13–15-year-olds in England between 2005 and 2012 found that 20 per cent could be classified as overweight and 7 per cent as obese. Girls were slightly more likely to be overweight, but boys more likely to be obese (8.3 per cent vs. 6.5 per cent). Irrespective of their actual weight, girls were more likely to rate themselves as too heavy compared to boys. This could be problematic for lower weight girls. Because they still see themselves as heavy, they may be inclined to lose more weight and veer towards being anorexic. For boys, however, the corresponding danger is that obese boys are less likely to recognize their condition. In fact, this survey found that nearly half (47 per cent) of the overweight or obese boys identified themselves as about the right weight or too light, compared to 32 per cent of girls.

The top three rows of Table 10 show data on overweight and obesity from the YRBS 2013 survey in the USA. Over 16 per cent of 14–18-year-olds describe themselves as overweight and at least 13 per cent as obese. Age changes over this period are rather small. There is also little gender difference in actually being overweight, and, as in the UK study, males are more likely actually to be obese in terms of the BMI criteria. However, and again similar to the UK study, females are much more likely to be concerned about it, with 36 per cent describing themselves as overweight compared to 26 per cent of males.

Eating disorders

Eating disorders comprise another set of internalizing problems prominent in adolescence. The bottom row of Table 10 shows data for what can be an indicator of eating disorder—namely, reporting

Table 10. Incidence (percentages) of three measures of overweight and obesity, and one of eating disorder, by grade and gender, in the USA, over a one-year period

Category / grade (age)	9 (14–15)	10 (15–16)	11 (16–17)	12 (17–18)	Male	Female
Overweight (BMI measure)	18	16	16	16	17	17
Described themselves as slightly or very overweight	30	30	33	32	26	36
Obese (BMI measure)	13	14	14	14	16	11
Did not eat for 24 hours during last 30 days	14	14	13	12	7	19

Source: USA data adapted from YRBS 2013 survey.

not eating for at least twenty-four hours in order to lose weight or keep from gaining weight. Here there are over twice as many females represented as males. There is a modest decline in this through the 14–18 age period. However, with nearly one in five female adolescents in the USA acting this way, it clearly remains a cause for concern.

Eating disorders can take a variety of forms, but there are two common types in adolescence. One is *anorexia nervosa*, which is defined as a lack of maintenance of a healthy body weight; obsessive fear of gaining weight or refusal to do so; and an unrealistic perception or non-recognition of the seriousness of low body weight. The other is *bulimia nervosa*, defined as recurrent binge eating followed by compensatory behaviours such as self-induced vomiting, use of laxatives, fasting, and over-exercising.

Causes of eating disorders are complex. There can be a family history of eating disorders, which might suggest either genetic factors or aspects of parenting. Being criticized about eating habits or parental pressure to eat more can contribute. There is an overlap with depression and with drug abuse. Eating disorders are also more frequent when there is pressure to be slim for certain activities, such as ballet or gymnastics.

Experiences of sexual or emotional abuse are a particular predictive factor for eating disorders. Controlling one's food intake, even in problematic ways, may be a way of trying to assert control over one's life when in other areas this has proved difficult or impossible. The following quote from an adolescent girl, quoted from *The Independent* newspaper in July 2015, illustrates this:

> My dad abused me when I was younger, so when I was little I had to grow up having to protect him even though he was supposed to be the one who looked after me. I feel as if I have had to grow up so

quickly and I never got to experience being a child. I have had an eating disorder for a long time now, and I think it is because I wanted to be in control of something. I never thought I would have the courage to speak to anyone about this.

Another factor can be cultural and media pressures, which to varying degrees extol an ideal of thinness. Feminist theorists in particular have argued that modern consumer-oriented societies have put pressure on women to have an ideal body by advertising beauty and dieting products, and using thin and even skinny models to illustrate these (see Figure 7). Traditionally it has been thought that this idealization of thinness is primarily a Western phenomenon. In developing countries where food is scarce, fatness might be valued and thinness seen as a sign of poverty or ill-health. However, recent evidence suggests that though there are many variations cross-culturally, the influences of Westernization and modernization have spread quite widely across the globe.

Eating disorders affect all ages and both genders, but for adolescent girls especially this can generate insecurity about their appearance at a time when self-consciousness about bodily changes at puberty and the imaginary audience phenomenon (Chapter 3) are at a peak. This is illustrated in a quote from another adolescent girl in *The Independent* newspaper:

> I have eaten too much and am feeling very guilty. I feel fat, ugly and worthless and want to make myself sick and self-harm. I always compare myself with other girls—especially models. I would like to go to the doctors but I am scared my parents are going to find out and force me to eat more. I know they are already worried that I'm not eating enough. I feel ashamed at school sometimes as people would judge me if they knew what I was doing.

There are a number of interactive websites around eating disorders, featuring blogs, discussion boards, etc. Here, like-minded

7. A model used by the clothing store Topshop which attracted criticism for being very skinny.

individuals with eating disorders can communicate and share feelings and experiences. These websites vary. In some, the focus will be on recovery and strategies for doing this. However, pro-anorexia websites can act to normalize the behaviour, and may include discussion and strategies about how to achieve an extremely low weight. They may provide some temporary comfort for an anorexic individual, but they are reinforcing the behaviour rather than contributing to a solution.

Interventions for eating disorders

Various kinds of counselling and therapy can be used to treat eating disorders. Cognitive behaviour therapy has been quite widely used. This is appropriate as it focuses on changing how the young person focuses on their situation and promotes more rational problem-solving and coping skills. It can be used to address body dissatisfaction, which may have been amplified by cultural or media pressures. Other kinds of therapy may be used. Family therapy can be appropriate if family factors are implicated in causing the problem. Nutrition counselling, self-help groups, and medication may also be advocated.

Historical changes

In the USA, the YRBS surveys from 1991 to 2013 showed a linear increase in proportions of young people who were overweight or obese. Although this problem seems to be getting worse, the same surveys found a linear decrease in numbers of those seriously considering and attempting suicide. But any improvements in the USA in such internalizing problems and mental health issues may be from an initially high level compared to other countries.

The Health Behaviour of School-aged Children (HBSC) surveys, carried out every four years, monitor well-being in 11-, 13-, and 15-year-olds. The surveys gather data from twenty-nine advanced economies (all European, plus USA and Canada). A composite measure of subjective well-being can be constructed from four domains: Life satisfaction; Peer and family relationships; Subjective education; and Subjective health. On this measure, using the 2009/10 data, the USA came lowest in subjective well-being. Compared with 2001/2 data, however, there were improvements in the USA in all four domains.

On these HBSC surveys, the UK came twentieth out of the twenty-nine countries in subjective well-being in 2009/10. Compared with 2001/2 data, there were improvements in three domains—but not in Subjective health, which got worse. There had been previous concerns about mental health, especially, of young people in the UK. A study of 15-year-olds in Scotland compared levels of mental health in 1987, 1999, and 2006. Scores got worse with time, most significantly for girls. Another report, funded by the Nuffield Foundation and based on sampling across the UK, used ratings from parents of 15-year-olds on the children's problem behaviours. Data were compared from 1974, 1986, and 1999. There were increases in emotional problems and conduct problems over the three time periods, for both sexes, but no consistent trend for hyperactivity. An update included further data obtained in 2004. On most measures there were small improvements from 1999 to 2004.

There are considerable cross-national differences in adolescent well-being from the HBSC data, with the Netherlands doing well on such indices and the USA and UK doing poorly. These differences and the time trends call out for explanation, but as yet our understanding is very limited. Analyses suggest that country level variables such as gross domestic product (GDP) or youth unemployment are not so important. For example, the USA has high GDP but does poorly on adolescent well-being. Rather, family factors and school factors such as levels of bullying have been pointed out as significant correlates of country differences.

Chapter 8
Sexual and romantic development, early parenthood, and emerging adulthood

As adolescents start to become reproductively mature at puberty, interest in sexual behaviour and partnerships increases. From associating primarily with same-sex friends during middle childhood, there is typically increased interest in relationships with the opposite sex from early to mid-teens onwards (Chapter 4). Some experience of same-sex sexual behaviours is also not uncommon, and a minority of adolescents will describe themselves as lesbian, gay, or bisexual. Intimate partnerships start to be formed, with sexual and romantic elements. Erikson's model (Chapter 3), which saw identity as being a main challenge of adolescence, saw intimacy as being the next normative challenge in development.

Attitudes to adolescent sexual behaviour

Human societies vary in attitudes to adolescent sexuality. This variation in attitude is true of traditional societies, although the review by Schlegel and Barry (Chapter 1) found that the majority were relatively tolerant. However, marriage occurs relatively early in traditional societies, and quite often marriage involves some financial transactions or property exchange. In these circumstances, there is more concern about adolescent sexual behaviour and especially their choice of partners.

In Western societies, attitudes to sexual matters on the whole have changed markedly during the 20th century. For example, masturbation is now seen as a normal activity with no harmful consequences, but for many years it was called self-abuse and in the first half of the 20th century it was seen as dangerous. *The Mothercraft Manual* in 1928 wrote that 'This is a bad habit...The habit, if left unchecked, may develop into a serious vice. The child's moral nature becomes perverted.' In contrast, Dr Spock's manual in 1976 stated that

> Some conscientious adolescents feel excessively guilty and worried about masturbation...If a child seems to be generally happy and successful, doing well in school, getting along with his friends, he can be told that all normal young people have these desires and that a great majority do masturbate.

In parallel, the age of first sexual intercourse has become earlier. For example, a study in Sweden asked people to recall the age of their first experience of sexual intercourse. For people born in the first decade of the 20th century, this was 18.6 years. For those born mid-century, it was 17.0 years. Ten years later, this had fallen to 16.0 years. In the UK, a survey in 1965 found that only about 18 per cent of 17-year-olds had experienced intercourse. Another survey in 1978 found a figure of about 45 per cent; and in a further survey in 1992 this had risen to 60 per cent.

Attitudes to premarital sexual intercourse have also become more permissive, although these changed more in the second half of the 20th century. The 1960s and 1970s especially saw a more relaxed attitude to sex before marriage in young people, perhaps influenced by the earlier age of puberty (Chapter 1) and increased availability of contraceptives. In a survey in the USA in 1969, only 21 per cent of Americans judged premarital sex not to be wrong, but by 1979 this had increased to 55 per cent. Of course, there remain variations in opinions about how acceptable this is, and it is generally seen as more acceptable within an affectionate relationship. There are cultural variations too even within modern industrialized societies. In Eastern countries such as Japan and Taiwan, attitudes are less permissive and the age of first intercourse tends to be later.

Development of sexual behaviours

With puberty usually starting at around 11–13 years, there is the potential for early sexual and romantic development. Some beginnings of this were delineated in a study in the Avon area around Bristol in England. As part of a broader survey, the researchers asked 11–12 and 12–13-year-olds about their experience of a range of intimate and sexual behaviours that had occurred during the last year with an unrelated person of the opposite sex. Only the 12–13-year-olds were asked about more intimate behaviours. Some findings are shown in Table 11. Early stages were holding hands and spending time alone together. Kissing on the mouth and cuddling were becoming more common by 12–13 years. However, very few, around 1 or 2 per cent, had fondled private parts, or had had oral sex or sexual intercourse.

Sexual experience increases rapidly from age 14 onwards. Data from a survey in 2008 by the Guttmacher Institute in the USA found that the percentage of adolescents who have had sexual intercourse starts from a very low level of 3 per cent before 14 years, but has risen to nearly 70 per cent by the end of the teenage years. The overall trends were very similar for males and females. The Youth Risk Behavior Surveillance (YRBS) survey in the USA of 14–18-year-olds in 2013 gave somewhat higher figures, with 5.6 per cent having intercourse before age 13. This survey also highlights large differences by ethnicity. For example, having intercourse before age 13 was reported by 3.3 per cent of White adolescents and 6.4 per cent of Hispanic adolescents, but by 14.0 per cent of Black adolescents.

Table 11. Percentages of early adolescents (boys/girls) who had experienced various intimate behaviours with the opposite sex over the previous year, in the Avon area of England, over a one-year period

	11–12 years	12–13 years
Held hands	27/21	43/39
Spent time alone	25/22	40/39
Kissed someone on the mouth	18/14	35/31
Been kissed on the mouth	19/15	34/29
Cuddled together	14/10	37/32
Lain down together	Not asked of younger adolescents	14/10
Been touched under your clothes		6/4
Touched someone under their clothes		7/3
Been undressed with private parts showing		2/1
Someone touched/ fondled your private parts		2/1
Touched/fondled someone's private parts		2/1
Had oral sex		1.2/0.5
Had sexual intercourse		1.0/0.3

Source: Andrea E. Waylen, Andrew Ness, Phil McGovern, Dieter Wolke, and Nicola Low (2010). Romantic and sexual behavior in young adolescents: repeated surveys in a population-based cohort. *The Journal of Early Adolescence*, June, 30/3, 432–43, Table 2. Reproduced with permission from *The Journal of Early Adolescence*.

While the extent of sexual experience in young people varies considerably, so also do related risk-taking aspects such as the number of sexual partners and the use of condoms. The YRBS survey of 14–18-year-olds found that some 15 per cent had had sexual intercourse with four or more persons. This increased from about 7 per cent at 15 years to 23 per cent by 18 years. The majority of adolescents used some form of birth control, usually a condom or pill, but nearly 14 per cent had not used any birth control method during their last sexual intercourse.

Sexual education for adolescents is an important and sometimes contentious topic. In the YRBS survey, 85 per cent of adolescents said they had been taught in school about AIDS and HIV. Besides the dangers of sexually transmitted diseases, comprehensive sexual education should include methods of contraception as well as discussion of respect and trust in intimate relationships. These are widely taught in many Western countries. In the USA there is a vocal movement proposing abstinence-only sex education. This argues that adolescents should abstain from sex before marriage, and contraceptive methods should not be taught as they would encourage premarital sex. Opponents of this point to the considerable rates of sexual intercourse that are clearly occurring well before marriage.

Romantic development

A romantic relationship can be defined as a mutually acknowledged dyadic relationship that involves expressions of affection with some degree of intensity. The proportion of adolescents who say they have a romantic partner increases with age, from around 40 per cent at age 13 to a clear majority by later adolescence. In addition, these relationships become longer lasting with age. For example, in one German study, the mean romantic relationship duration was found to be 3.9 months at 13 years, 5.1 months at 15 years, and 11.8 months at 17 years, jumping to 21.3 months by 21 years.

A study in Canada of 12–15-year-olds suggested four stages in the development of romantic relationships. This study focused on heterosexual relationships. The first stage is of mixing mainly in same-sex friendship groups (Chapter 4). The second stage they called mixed-gender affiliative activities. This included hanging around in mixed-sex groups; and going to clubs, dances, and sports activities with both boys and girls. These experiences provide a gentle introduction to mixed-sex relationships, and younger or more shy adolescents can observe what slightly older or more confident individuals are doing. While these mixed-sex affiliative activities continue, older adolescents move into dating activities. This is typically in groups to start with, but sometimes quite small groups—for example, a couple of friends. In the fourth stage, the adolescent is involved in dyadic dating and clearly has a specific romantic partner. This study found that adolescents from Asian origin families were later in dating and forming romantic relationships than those classified as of European or Caribbean origin, probably because of different cultural and familial expectations.

Lesbian and gay adolescents

Although most romantic relationships are heterosexual, a significant minority are not. The Guttmacher Institute survey of 13–20-year-olds in the USA found that 3 per cent of males and 8 per cent of females reported their sexual orientation as homosexual or bisexual. A somewhat larger number, 4 per cent of males and 12 per cent of females, reported having had some same-sex experience.

Attitudes towards homosexual behaviour vary very greatly. The review of traditional societies by Schlegel and Barry (Chapter 1) found that about two-thirds had rather tolerant attitudes towards homosexual acts during adolescence. In some societies it was quite normative and ritualized among all-male groups. However, homosexual behaviours were often of a casual or transient nature. They did not necessarily lead to homosexual orientation in adults, and instead could often be seen as a kind of youthful experimentation. This was available until they were ready for heterosexual intercourse and then marriage. In Western societies, tolerance of homosexuality has increased greatly in recent decades. However, it remains discriminated against or even is illegal in some countries, including many modern African countries.

Initial awareness of same-sex attraction can start as early as 10–15 years, so at much the same time as heterosexual interests start to develop. However, consciously labelling oneself as gay or lesbian typically occurs towards the end of this period, around 15 years. 'Coming out', or disclosing a different sexual identity, may be delayed another year or so, or sometimes much longer, due to uncertainty about how this may be perceived and reacted to. A gay or lesbian adolescent, or someone who is bisexual or questioning their sexual identity, has to think about the consequences of coming out, including not only reactions of friends and family, but also wider aspects such as social customs, religious opinions, and legal issues—for example, whether there is the possibility of recognized gay partnerships or marriage. These vary greatly in different countries and are still changing rapidly, as seen by the broad legalization of gay marriage in the USA at the time of writing.

Gender dysphoria

While most people experience little doubt about their gender, some can experience unhappiness with their physical sex and/or gender role. This is referred to as *gender dysphoria*. Although this can occur in childhood, it is a more stable condition in adolescence. A small number of adolescents may wish to consider changing gender. Common clinical procedures here are first to delay puberty, using gonadotropin releasing hormone analogues. This is a reversible procedure that gives the young person more time to consider their options. If they wish to proceed (usually after age 16) then cross-sex hormones can be used to change bodily appearance, and the young person is encouraged to live in their new gender role. By (usually) age 18, and if various eligibility criteria are met, then the irreversible process of gender re-assignment surgery may take place.

Activities within romantic relationships

A study in the midwestern USA looked at activities engaged in within romantic relationships at grades 5, 8, and 11 (about 10–11, 13–14, and 16–17 years old). This study again focused on heterosexual relationships. Those who had such a relationship were asked which of thirty-two activities they had engaged in together. Table 12 shows the findings for the thirteen activities engaged in overall by at least half of respondents. Talking about personal things, which is clearly a measure of intimacy and trust, increased greatly with age, more so than talking about non-personal things. Most activities showed an increase with age, and many of them showed a positive relationship with a measure of romantic relationship satisfaction. Interestingly, emails and instant messaging peaked at grade 8. This survey was published in 2012 but the date of the survey is not given. A comparable survey now might well feature social networking activities more prominently (Chapter 5).

Dating violence

Most early romantic and dating experiences are positive (Table 12). But like all relationships, dating can have a dark side. There can be physical violence, sexual violence and coercion, and emotional abuse. Recently, technology is playing an increasing role in dating violence, as in the example of unwanted sexting (see next section). These activities are likely to lead to a breakup in the relationship, but this does not always happen. Some young people will stay in an abusive relationship because they hope it will improve. Others will stay in it because they have experienced

Table 12. Percentage of adolescents with an opposite-sex romantic partner who engaged in various activities, at different grade levels, in the USA

Activity / grade (age)	5 (10–11)	8 (13–14)	11 (16–17)
Talk on the telephone	78	93	90
Talk about non-personal things	53	80	89
Talk about personal things	38	69	90
Listen to music	43	65	87
Talk in school	66 [no significant grade differences]		
Go to each other's houses after school/ weekends	30	61	92
Watch TV	38	47	91
Do an outdoor activity	60 [no significant grade differences]		
Hang out at school when there is free time	59 [no significant grade differences]		
Go to a sporting event	40	66	63
Go to dances	18	69	69
Go to the movies, just the two of you	18	55	69
Write emails/instant messages	23	73	51

Source: Wendy Carlson and Amanda J. Rose (2012). Brief report: activities in heterosexual romantic relationships. Grade differences and associations with relationship satisfaction. *Journal of Adolescence*, February, 35/1, 219–24. Reprinted with permission from Elsevier.

earlier abuse as a child, and they expect this kind of behaviour in a relationship—their model of relationships is one that includes abusive behaviours within it. Either way, there is a high probability of the abuse continuing if they do stay in it.

Some data from the YRBS data in the USA for the 2013 survey is shown in Table 13. This shows that some 10 per cent of 14–18-year-olds say that they have experienced dating violence in the last year. This percentage increases with age. Some males experience dating violence, but it is nearly twice as frequent in females. Prevalence rates do depend very much on how questions are asked. A study in Italy and Canada with 14–16-year-olds found high prevalence rates of around 30 per cent and 33 per cent in the two countries. Here, adolescents were asked how often they had experienced different kinds of physical dating aggression in their current or past dating relationship. The prevalence rates included rarely or more often, and covered any of nine categories including pushing (the most common), hitting, spitting, choking, pulling hair, biting, arm twisting, throwing an object, and slamming against a wall.

Sexting

A recent activity which has aroused some concern is *sexting*. This has been defined as the sending, receiving, and forwarding of sexually explicit messages, images, or photos to others through electronic means, primarily between mobile phones. As early romantic relationships develop, a boy may ask a girlfriend for such photos of herself (or vice versa, but it is usually the former way around). In Europe, the EU Kids Online project (Chapter 5) reported that 15 per cent of 11–16-year-olds had received peer to peer sexual messages or images, and 3 per cent said they had sent or posted such images themselves.

This in itself may be harmless. But while it is often voluntary, some (usually female) adolescents may feel pressurized or coerced

Table 13. Incidence (percentages) of adolescents experiencing physical dating violence, by grade and gender, in the USA, over a one-year period

Category / grade (age)	9 (14–15)	10 (15–16)	11 (16–17)	12 (17–18)	Male	Female
Experienced physical dating violence in the previous 12 months	9	10	10	12	7	13

Source: USA data adapted from YRBS 2013 survey.

to send such images or *sexts* in order to try and avoid an argument or relationship breakup. Also, in mid-adolescence romantic relationships are not long-lasting—typically a matter of months. When the relationship ends, or if it becomes abusive, then sexually explicit texts or photos may be shared very widely without the girl's consent. If this is done with the intention of humiliating the person depicted, it has been called *revenge porn*. This can be a hugely embarrassing experience, sometimes leading to depression or even suicidal thoughts (Chapter 6). A number of countries have passed laws against revenge porn.

Education about the risks in sexting is important. In the UK, the Child Exploitation and Online Protection Centre (CEOP) has produced films, resources, and guidelines for schools about sexting. This includes a short film, *Exposed*, which portrays the strong negative effects of an unwanted and abusive sexting experience. Many websites used by young people include a ClickCEOP button to report this or other kinds of sexual abuse to a team of specialist child protection advisors.

Teenage pregnancies and early parenthood

With rates of sexual intercourse rising rapidly from around age 15, inevitably some pregnancies will ensue. In many traditional

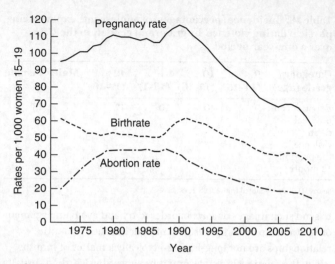

8. **Changes in teen pregnancy and abortion rates in the USA over a forty-year period.**

societies, having a child or children while in the later teens would be common or even normative. However, in the modern Western economies, teenage pregnancies are usually seen as a cause for concern. The survey in the USA by the Guttmacher Institute found that 82 per cent of pregnancies in the 15–19-year age period were unplanned. Some teen parents can function well, especially if supported by their own parents. But some teen mothers will lack adequate social and financial support, and many drop out of school or college early. The infant mortality rate is higher for teen mothers. Also, statistically, the longer term prognosis for their child is less good on a range of educational and health indicators.

Figure 8 shows statistics from the USA for pregnancy, birth, and abortion rates, over a recent forty-year period, for 15–19-year-olds. From a high in 1991, pregnancy rates had fallen by about a half by 2010. About 60 per cent of teen pregnancies resulted in birth; with 26 per cent resulting in abortion; and 15 per cent in miscarriage. Rates of birth, and of abortion, have also dropped considerably in the last twenty years.

Why has there been this decrease? A major factor appears to be more contraceptive use. The Guttmacher Institute survey indicated that the use of contraceptives during first sex by females aged 15–19 years increased from 48 per cent in 1982 to 78 per cent in 2010. The condom is the most used contraceptive device. Besides easier availability, the AIDS epidemic in the later 20th century is thought to have been a factor in increased contraceptive use.

By international standards, the USA has a high level of teenage births. For 2012 the figure was 29.4 births per 1,000 women aged 15–19 years. In the UK, the corresponding figure was 19.7 births. The UK figure too has seen a considerable drop in recent years (in 2004 it was 26.9). The average rate in the EU was 12.6. Within the EU, the UK came fourth highest, below Bulgaria, Romania, and Slovakia. The lowest rates, all below 5 per 1,000, were in Denmark, Slovenia, and the Netherlands.

Emerging adulthood

Adolescence is normally thought of as leading directly to adulthood. In traditional societies, this generally has been the case (Chapter 1). However, in modern industrial societies, the period of adolescence has been seen as extended due to a longer period of schooling; and delays in leaving home, marrying, and having children. For example in the USA, the median age of marriage in the 1950s was around 20 years for women and 22 years for men. But by 2012, this had risen to about 27 years for women and 28.5 years for men. There have been similar trends in many European countries and other industrialized countries such as Australia, Canada, and Japan.

Jeffrey Arnett proposed in 2000 that in recent decades and in the modern Western economies, it makes sense to consider a period of *emerging adulthood*. This would be from around 18 years through to 25, or possibly 29 years. He based this argument on both subjective and objective indicators.

The subjective indicator is whether someone feels they have reached adulthood. Few adolescents answer 'yes' to this question, but most people in their 30s do. However, in the 18–25 year age range, most people in the USA answer 'yes and no', indicating some in-between status. This is borne out by objective indicators. The main indicators are summarized for the USA in Table 14. Most adolescents are living with a parent or parents and attending school or college; few have a child themselves; and very few are married. By their 30s, this is reversed. Very few are living with parents or still at college. The majority are married and have a child or children. The emerging adulthood period describes this period of transition as taking place mainly between 18 and 25 years.

Unlike most adolescents, emerging adults have full legal rights (for example, to drive, to serve in the armed forces, and to vote). They have moved well past the changes associated with puberty and are fully reproductively mature. They are typically becoming

Table 14. Some characteristics (by percentage) of adolescents and of adults in their 30s, from US data

	Adolescence [10–18 years]		Adulthood [30+ years]
Living in parent's home	92	Emerging adulthood	<10
Attending school or college	95		7
Have a child	10		75
Married	2		75

Sources: Data from National Center for Education Statistics for 2012; and United States Census Bureau, 2015.

fully independent, financially and psychologically, from parents. However, in one sense, emerging adulthood does resemble an extension of adolescence. This is in terms of identity development and the psychosocial moratorium (Chapter 3). Arnett argues that much of this now takes place in the emerging adult period. This would be particularly true of love relationships, and career choices. The emerging adult may experience several serious romantic involvements before settling into marriage or a sustained partnership, often involving children. Also, they may move through several short-term jobs while perhaps also pursuing further qualifications, before settling on a more definite career course.

Adolescence in comparative perspective: concluding remarks

Adolescence varies in different cultures and at different historical times. It is viewed in different ways, and young people face different challenges and opportunities in their transition to adult life. Even in recent decades, there have been noticeable changes in the salience of issues such as mental health problems and obesity. Currently, youth unemployment is a concern in advanced economies. The spread of mobile phones and the internet has affected everyone, but at the time of writing the growth in social networking sites has been especially powered by adolescents; for this generation at least they are the digital natives. Nevertheless, there are common features across the adolescent experience, wherever and whenever it happens. All adolescents experience the physical changes of puberty, and we are learning much more now about the associated brain changes and the psychological changes in areas such as risk-taking, as well as the importance of the peer group. Adolescence provides a fascinating set of issues for researchers. It can be a challenging period for parents, and an often tumultuous period for the young people themselves. However, most of them negotiate this period successfully, moving on to emerging adulthood and a productive adult life.

Publisher's acknowledgements

We are grateful for permission to include the following copyright material in this book:

Extracts from Emily Dugan, 'Exclusive: eating disorders soar among teens—and social media is to blame', *The Independent*, Sunday, 26 January 2014. (<http://www.independent.co.uk/life-style/health-and-families/health-news/exclusive-eating-disorders-soar-among-teens-and-social-media-is-to-blame-9085500.html>), reproduced with permission from *The Independent*

The publisher and author have made every effort to trace and contact all copyright holders before publication. If notified, the publisher will be pleased to rectify any errors or omissions at the earliest opportunity.

Further reading

Chapter 1: Adolescence as a life stage

Ariès, P. (1962). *Centuries of childhood: a social history of the family.* New York: Vintage Books.

Arnett, J. (1995). Broad and narrow socialization: the family in the context of a cultural theory. *Journal of Marriage and the Family,* 57, 617–28.

Arnett, J. (1999). Adolescent storm and stress, reconsidered. *American Psychologist,* 54, 317–26.

Belsky, J. (2012). The development of human reproductive strategies: progress and prospects. *Current Directions in Psychological Science,* 21, 310–16.

Blakemore, S.-J. and Mills, K.L. (2014). Is adolescence a sensitive period for sociocultural processing? *Annual Review of Psychology,* 65, 187–207.

Freeman, D. (1999). *The fateful hoaxing of Margaret Mead.* Boulder, CO: Westview Press.

Hanawalt, B.A. (1992). Historical descriptions and prescriptions for adolescence. *Journal of Family History,* 17, 341–51.

Konner, M. (2010). *The evolution of childhood.* Cambridge, MA: Harvard University Press.

Mead, M. (1928). *Coming of age in Samoa.* New York: Morrow.

Raum, O. (1940). *Chaga childhood.* London: Oxford University Press.

Schlegel, A. and Barry, H., III (1991). *Adolescence: an anthropological inquiry.* New York: Free Press.

Tonkinson, R. (1978). *The Mardujara Aborigines.* New York: Holt, Rinehart and Winston.

Weisfeld, G. and Janisse, H.C. (2005). Some functional aspects of human adolescence. In B.J. Ellis and D.F. Bjorklund (eds), *Origins of the Social Mind: Evolutionary Psychology and Child Development*. New York: Guilford Publications, pp. 189–218.

Zerjal, T. et al. (2003). The genetic legacy of the Mongols. *American Journal of Human Genetics*, 72, 717–21.

An interesting archive of material on Mead's work in Samoa, including photographs, letters and field notes, is available at www.loc.gov/exhibits/mead/field-samoa.html

Chapter 2: Puberty—body and brain changes

Burnett, S., Sebastian, C., Kadosh, K.C., and Blakemore, S.-J. (2011). The social brain in adolescence: evidence from functional magnetic resonance imaging and behavioural studies. *Neuroscience and Biobehavioral Reviews*, 35, 1654–64.

Chen, F.-F., Wang, Y.-F., and Mi, J. (2014). Timing and secular trend of pubertal development in Beijing girls. *World Journal of Pediatrics*, 10, 74–9.

Hermann-Giddens, M., Slora, E., and Wasserman, R. (1997). Secondary sexual characteristics and menses in young girls. *Paediatrics*, 99, 505–12.

Magnusson, D., Stattin, H., and Allen, V.L. (1985). Biological maturation and social development: a longitudinal study of some adjustment processes from mid-adolescence to adulthood. *Journal of Youth and Adolescence*, 14, 267–83.

Moffitt, T. (1993). Adolescence-limited and life-course-persistent antisocial behavior: a developmental taxonomy. *Psychological Review*, 100, 674–701.

Peper, J.S. and Dahl, R.E. (2013). The teenage brain: surging hormones—brain–behavior interactions during puberty. *Current Directions in Psychological Science*, 22, 134–9.

Tanner, J.M. (1978; 2nd edn 1990). *Fetus into man: physical growth from conception to maturity*. Cambridge, MA: Harvard University Press.

Chapter 3: Formal operational thought, moral development, and identity

Crocetti, E., Klimstra, T.A., Hale, W.W., III, Kroot, H.M., and Meueus, W. (2013). Impact of early adolescent externalizing behaviors on identity development in middle to late adolescence: a prospective 7-year longitudinal study. *Journal of Youth and Adolescence*, 42, 1745–58.

Elkind, D. (1967). Egocentrism in adolescence. *Child Development*, 38, 1025–34.

Erikson, E. (1968). *Identity: youth and crisis*. London: Faber.

Gilligan, C. (1982). *In a different voice: psychological theory and women's development*. Cambridge, MA: Harvard University Press.

Inhelder, B. and Piaget, J. (1958; orig. 1955). *The growth of logical thinking from childhood to adolescence*. London: Routledge and Kegan Paul.

Kohlberg, L. (1976). Moral stages and moralization: the cognitive-developmental approach. In T. Lickona (ed.), *Moral development and behavior*. New York: Holt, Rinehart and Winston.

Kunnen, E.S., Sappa, V., van Geert, P.L.C., and Bonica, L. (2008). The shapes of commitment development in emerging adulthood. *Journal of Adult Development*, 15, 113–31.

Marcia, J.E. (1966). Development and validation of ego-identity status. *Journal of Personality and Social Psychology*, 3, 551–8.

Piaget, J. (1972). Intellectual evolution from adolescence to adulthood. *Human Development*, 15, 1–12.

Rivas-Drake, D. et al. (2014). Ethnic and racial identity in adolescence: implications for psychosocial, academic, and health outcomes. *Child Development*, 85, 40–57.

Sebastian, C., Burnett, S., and Blakemore, S.-J. (2008). Development of the self-concept during adolescence. *Trends in Cognitive Sciences*, 12, 441–6.

Chapter 4: Relationship changes—parents and peers

Amichai-Hamburger, Y., Kingsbury, M., and Schneider, B.H. (2013). Friendship: an old concept with a new meaning? *Computers in Human Behavior*, 29, 33–9.

Cairns, R.B., Leung, M.-C., Buchanan, L., and Cairns, B.D. (1995). Friendships and social networks in childhood and adolescence: fluidity, reliability, and interrelations. *Child Development*, 66, 1330–45.

Closson, L.M. (2009). Status and gender differences in early adolescents' descriptions of popularity. *Social Development*, 18, 412–26.

Crone, E.A. (2013). Considerations of fairness in the adolescent brain. *Child Development Perspectives*, 7, 97–103.

Dunphy, D.C. (1963). The social structure of urban adolescent peer groups. *Sociometry*, 26, 230–46.

Juang, L.P., Lerner, J.V., McKinney, J.P., and von Eye, A. (1999). The goodness of fit in autonomy timetable expectations between Asian-American late adolescents and their parents. *International Journal of Behavioral Development*, 23, 1023–48.

Kelley, P., Lockley, S.W., Foster, R.G., and Kelley, J. (2015). Synchronizing education to adolescent biology: 'let teens sleep, start school later'. *Learning, Media and Technology*, 40, 210–26.

Lam, C.B., McHale, S.M., and Crouter, A.C. (2014). Time with peers from middle childhood to late adolescence: developmental course and adjustment correlates. *Child Development*, 85, 1677–93.

Laursen, B., Cox, K.C., and Collins, W.A. (1998). Reconsidering changes in parent–child conflict across adolescence: a meta-analysis. *Child Development*, 69, 817–32.

Lichtwarck-Aschoff, A., Kunnen, S.E., and van Geert, P.L.C. (2009). Here we go again: a dynamic systems perspective on emotional rigidity across parent–adolescent conflicts. *Developmental Psychology*, 45, 1364–75.

Nucci, L., Smetana, J., Araki, N., Nakaue, M., and Comer, J. (2014). Japanese adolescents' disclosure and information management with parents. *Child Development*, 85, 901–7.

Pomerantz, E.M. and Wang, Q. (2009). The role of parental control in children's development in Western and East Asian countries. *Current Directions in Psychological Science*, 18, 285–9.

Rossi, A.H. and Rossi, P.H. (1991). *Of human bonding: parent–child relations across the life course*. New York: de Gruyter.

Sebastian, C., Viding, E., Williams, K.D., and Blakemore, S.-J. (2010). Social brain development and the affective consequences of ostracism in adolescence. *Brain and Cognition*, 72, 134–45.

Smetana, J. and Gaines, C. (1999). Adolescent–parent conflict in middle-class African American families. *Child Development*, 70, 1447–63.

Smith, P.K. (2014). *Understanding school bullying: its nature and prevention strategies*. London: Sage.

Timmons, A.C. and Margolin, G. (2015). Family conflict, mood, and adolescents' daily school problems: moderating roles of internalizing and externalizing symptoms. *Child Development*, 86, 241–58.

Chapter 5: Youth culture—leisure pursuits and the cyberworld

Anderson, C.A., Shibuya, A., Ihori, N., Swing, E.L., Bushman, B.J., Sakamoto, A., Rothstein, H.R., and Saleem, M. (2010). Violent video game effects on aggression, empathy, and prosocial behavior in Eastern and Western countries: a meta-analytic review. *Psychological Bulletin*, 136, 151–73.

Best, J.R. (2013). Exergaming in youth: effects on physical and cognitive health. *Zeitschrift für Psychologie*, 221, 72–8.

Blumberg, F., Blades, M., and Oates, C. (2013). Youth and new media: the appeal and educational ramifications of digital game play for children and adolescents. *Zeitschrift für Psychologie*, 221, 67–71.

boyd, d. (2014). *It's complicated: the social life of networked teens*. New Haven & London: Yale University Press.

Danish, S.J., Taylor, T.E., and Fazio, R.J. (2003). Enhancing adolescent development through sports and leisure. In G.R. Adams and M.D. Berzonsky (eds), *Blackwell Handbook of Adolescence*, pp. 92–108. Oxford: Blackwell.

Dolev-Cohen, M. and Barak, A. (2013). Adolescents' use of Instant Messaging as a means of emotional relief. *Computers in Human Behavior*, 29, 58–63.

Greenberg, B.S. and Mastro, D.E. (2008). Children, race ethnicity and media. In S.L. Calvert and B.J. Wilson (eds), *The handbook of children, media, and development*. Oxford: Blackwell.

Larson, R.W. (2000). Toward a psychology of positive youth development. *American Psychologist*, 55, 170–83.

Livingstone, S., Haddon, L., Görzig, A., and Ólafsson, K. (2011). *Final report: EU kids online II*. London: EU Kids Online, LSE.

Ofcom (2014). *Children and parents: media use and attitudes report*. London: Office of Communications.

Punamaki, R.-J., Wallenius, M., Hölltö, H., Nygård, C.-H., and Rimpelä, A. (2009). The associations between information and communication technology (ICT) and peer and parent relations in early adolescence. *International Journal of Behavioral Development*, 33, 556–64.

Useful websites

Kaiser Foundation, www.kff.org

Ofcom, www.ofcom.org.uk

Pew Research Center, www.pewinternet.org

UK Safer Internet Day, www.saferinternet.org.uk

Further reading

Chapter 6: Risk-taking, antisocial behaviour, and delinquency

Burnett, S., Bault, N., Coricelli, G., and Blakemore, S.-J. (2010). Adolescents' heightened risk-seeking in a probabilistic gambling task. *Cognitive Development*, 25, 183–96.

Byrnes, J.P., Miller, D.C., and Schafer, W.D. (1999). Gender differences in risk-taking: a meta-analysis. *Psychological Bulletin*, 125, 367–83.

Carroll, A., Houghton, S., Hattie, J., and Durkin, D. (1999). Adolescent reputation enhancement: differentiating delinquent, nondelinquent and at-risk youths. *Journal of Child Psychology & Psychiatry*, 40, 593–606.

Cebulla, A. and Tomaszewski, W. (2009). *Risky behaviour and social activities*. Research Report DCSF-RR173. London: Department for Children, Schools and Families.

Chein, J., Albert, D., O'Brien, L., Uckert, K., and Steinberg, L. (2011). Peers increase adolescent risk taking by enhancing activity in the brain's reward circuitry. *Developmental Science*, 14, F1–10.

Ellis, B.J., del Guidice, M., Dishion, T.J., Figueredo, A.J., Gray, P., Griskevicius, V., Hawley, P.H., Jacobs, W.J., James, J., Volk, A.A., and Wilson, D.S. (2012). The evolutionary basis of risk taking behavior: implications for science, policy, and practice. *Developmental Psychology*, 48, 598–623.

Encarta World English Dictionary (1999). London: Bloomsbury Publishing.

Farrington, D.P. (1995). The development of offending and anti-social behaviour from childhood: key findings from the Cambridge Study in Delinquent Development. *Journal of Child Psychology & Psychiatry*, 36, 929–64.

Gardner, M. and Steinberg, L. (2005). Peer influence on risk taking, risk preference, and risky decision making in adolescence and adulthood: an experimental study. *Developmental Psychology*, 41, 625–35.

Gatti, U., Tremblay, R.E., Vitaro, F., and McDuff, P. (2005). Youth gangs, delinquency and drug use. *Journal of Child Psychology & Psychiatry*, 46, 1178–90.

Hayward, R. and Sharp, C. (2005). *Young people, crime and antisocial behaviour: findings from the 2003 Crime and Justice Survey*. London: Home Office, Findings 245.

Hirschi, T. (1969). *Causes of delinquency*. Berkeley: University of California Press.

Lim, S.S., Chan, Y.H., Vadrevu, S., and Basnyat, I. (2013). Managing peer relationships online: investigating the use of Facebook by juvenile delinquents and youths-at-risk. *Computers in Human Behavior*, 29, 8–15.

Moffitt, T. (1993). Adolescence-limited and life-course-persistent antisocial behavior: a developmental taxonomy. *Psychological Review*, 100, 674–701.

Monaghan, K.C., Steinberg, L., and Cauffman, E. (2009). Affiliation with antisocial peers, susceptibility to peer influence, and antisocial behavior during the transition to adulthood. *Developmental Psychology*, 45, 1520–30.

Pagani, L., Tremblay, R.E., Vitaro, F., Kerr, M., and McDuff, P. (1998). The impact of family transition on the development of delinquency in adolescent boys. *Journal of Child Psychology & Psychiatry*, 39, 489–99.

Pagani, L., Boulerice, B., Vitaro, F., and Tremblay, R.E., (1999). Effects of poverty on academic failure and delinquency in boys. *Journal of Child Psychology & Psychiatry*, 40, 1209–19.

Shin, W. and Ismail, N. (2014). Exploring the role of parents and peers in young adolescents' risk taking on social networking sites. *Cyberpsychology, Behavior, and Social Networking*, 17, 578–83.

Steinberg L., Albert, D., Cauffman, E., Banich, M., Graham, S., and Woolard, J. (2008). Age differences in sensation seeking and impulsivity as indexed by behavior and self-report: evidence for a dual systems model. *Developmental Psychology*, 44, 1764–78.

Van Petegem, S., Soenens, B., Vansteenkiste, M., and Beyers, W. (2015). Rebels with a cause? Adolescent defiance from the perspective of reactance theory and self-determination theory. *Child Development*, 86, 903–18.

Wolf, L.K., Wright, N.D., Kilford, E.J., Dolan, R.J., and Blakemore, S.-J. (2013). Developmental changes in effects of risk and valence on adolescent decision-making. *Cognitive Development*, 28, 290–9.

Youth Risk Behavior Surveillance (2013). Survey. US Department of Health and Human Services: Centers for Disease Control and Prevention.

Chapter 7: Internalizing disorders and adolescent mental health

Antilla, K., Antilla, M., Kurki, M., Hätönen, H., Marttunen, M., and Välimäki, M. (2015). Concerns and hopes among adolescents attending adolescent psychiatric outpatient clinics. *Child and Adolescent Mental Health*, 20, 81–8.

Bradshaw, J., Martorano, B., Natali, L., and de Neubourg, C. (2013). Children's subjective well-being in rich countries. *Child Indicators Research*, 6, 619–35.

Coleman, J. (1978). Current contradictions in adolescent theory. *Journal of Youth and Adolescence*, 7, 1–11.

Gradinger, P., Strohmeier, D., and Spiel, C. (2009). Traditional bullying and cyberbullying: identification of risk groups for adjustment problems. *Zeitschrift für Psychologie / Journal of Psychology*, 217, 205–13.

The Independent (2015). Eating disorders soar among teens—and social media is to blame. 3 July. www.independent.co.uk/life-style/health-and-families/health-news/exclusive-eating-disorders-soar-among-teens--and-social-media-is-to-blame-9085500.html

Jackson, S.E., Johnson, F., Croker, H., and Wardle, J. (2015). Weight perceptions in a population sample of English adolescents: cause for celebration or concern? *International Journal of Obesity*, 39, 1488–93.

Karch, D.L., Logan, J., Daniel, D.D., Floyd, C.F., and Vagi, K.J. (2013). Precipitating circumstances of suicide among youth aged 10–17 years by sex: data from the National Violent Death Reporting System, 16 states, 2005–2008. *Journal of Adolescent Health*, 53, S51–3.

Larson, R. and Ham, M. (1993). Stress and 'storm and stress' in early adolescence: the relationship of negative events with dysphoric affect. *Developmental Psychology*, 29, 130–40.

Martorano, B., Natali, L., de Neubourg, C., and Bradshaw, J. (2014). Children's well-being in advanced economies in the late 2000s. *Social Indicators Research*, 118, 247–83.

Nuffield Foundation (2009). *Time trends in adolescent well-being: update 2009*. London: Nuffield Foundation.

Robinson, J.P., Espelage, D.L., and Rivers, I. (2013). Developmental trends in peer victimization and emotional distress in LGB and heterosexual youth. *Pediatrics*, 131, 423–30.

Rutter, M., Graham, P., Chadwick, O., and Yule, W. (1976). Adolescent turmoil: fact or fiction? *Journal of Child Psychology and Psychiatry*, 17, 35–56.

Swami, V. (2015). Cultural influences on body size ideals: unpacking the impact of Westernization and modernization. *European Psychologist*, 20, 44–51.

Youth Risk Behavior Surveillance (2013). Survey. US Department of Health and Human Services: Centers for Disease Control and Prevention.

Chapter 8: Sexual and romantic development, early parenthood, and emerging adulthood

Arnett, J. (2000). Emerging adulthood: a theory of development from the late teens through the twenties. *American Psychologist*, 57, 774–83.

Arnett, J. (2014). *Emerging adulthood: the winding road from the late teens through the twenties*, 2nd edn. New York: Oxford University Press.

Carlson, W. and Rose, A.J. (2012). Brief report: activities in heterosexual romantic relationships. Grade differences and associations with relationship satisfaction. *Journal of Adolescence*, 35, 219–24.

Centers for Disease Control and Prevention (2011). *Sexual identity, sex of sexual contacts, and health risk behaviors among students in grades 9-12—youth risk behavior surveillance, selected sites, United States, 2001-2009.* MMWR, 60, 1–133.

Connolly, J., Craig, W., Goldberg, A., and Pepler, D. (2004). Mixed-gender groups, dating, and romantic relationships in early adolescence. *Journal of Research on Adolescence*, 14, 185–207.

De Vries, A.L.C. and Cohen-Kettenis, P.T. (2012). Clinical management of gender dysphoria in children and adolescents: the Dutch approach. *Journal of Homosexuality*, 59, 301–20.

Floyd, F.J. and Bakeman, R. (2006). Coming-out across the life course: implications for age and historical context. *Archives of Sexual Behavior*, 35, 287–96.

Guttmacher Institute (2014). American teens sexual and reproductive health. Fact Sheet, May.

Klettke, B., Hallford, D.J., and Mellor, D.J. (2014). Sexting prevalence and correlates: a systematic literature review. *Clinical Psychology Review*, 34, 44–53.

Nocentini, A., Menesini, E., Pastorelli, C., Connolly, J., Pepler, D., and Craig, W. (2011). Physical dating aggression in adolescence: cultural and gender invariance. *European Psychologist*, 16, 278–87.

Office for National Statistics (2014). International comparisons of teenage births. www.ons.gov.uk

Rivers, I. and Gordon, K. (2010). 'Coming out', context and reason: first disclosure of sexual orientation and its consequences. *Psychology and Sexuality*, 1, 21–33.

Seiffge-Krenke, I. (2003). Testing theories of romantic development from adolescence to young adulthood: evidence of a developmental sequence. *International Journal of Behavioral Development*, 27, 519–31.

Smith, P.K., Cowie, H., and Blades, M. (2015). *Understanding children's development*, 6th edn. Chichester: Wiley-Blackwell.

Sundet, J.M., Magnus, P., Kvalem, I.L., Samuelsen, S.O., and Bakketeig, L.S. (1992). Secular trends and sociodemographic regularities of coital debut age in Norway. *Archives of Sexual Behavior*, 21, 241–52.

Waylen, A.E., Ness, A., McGovern, P., Wolke, D., and Low, N. (2010). Romantic and sexual behavior in young adolescents. *Journal of Early Adolescence*, 30, 432–43.

Wellings, K. (2009). Poverty or promiscuity: sexual behaviour in global context. Paper presented at Training Course in Sexual and Reproductive Health Research, Geneva. www.gfmer.ch/Medical_education_En/PGC_SRH_2009/Poverty_promiscuity_Wellings_2009.htm

Useful websites

National Center for Education Statistics, nces.ed.gov

United States Census Bureau, www.census.gov

Index